Portfolio Management and Ethical and Professional Standards: CFA Level 2 2026

Azhar ul Haque Sario

Copyright

First Printing, 2025

Azhar.sario@hotmail.co.uk

ORCID: https://orcid.org/0009-0004-8629-830X
LinkedIn: https://www.linkedin.com/in/azharulhaquesario/

Disclaimer: This book is free from AI use. The cover was designed in Canva.

Disclaimer: This publication is an independent work. It is not affiliated with, endorsed, or sponsored by the CFA Institute. This book is produced under the principles of nominative fair use for educational and preparatory purposes.

Contents

Subject 1: Portfolio Management

Economics and Investment Markets

The Three Levers of Market Value
Imagine you're thinking about buying a small, local coffee shop. What makes it valuable to you? At its core, its value comes down to a few key things: how much profit you expect it to make in the future, when you'll get that profit, and how certain you are about actually receiving it. This simple coffee shop analogy is a fantastic way to understand the complex world of market valuation for any asset, whether it's a stock, a bond, or a piece of real estate.

The market value of any investment is fundamentally a reflection of its future cash flows, discounted back to what they're worth today. Think of it like this: a dollar promised to you a year from now is worth less than a dollar in your hand today. Why? Because you could invest that dollar today and earn a return on it. This concept is the bedrock of finance.

For any broad economic factor—like a change in government policy, a technological breakthrough, or a global pandemic—to actually move the needle on market prices, it must pull one of three fundamental levers. It has to change:

The default-free interest rate, which is like the base-level rent you charge for lending out your money.

The expected cash flows, which is the amount of money you think the investment will generate.

The risk premium, which is the extra return you demand for taking on uncertainty.

Let's break these down one by one, because understanding them is like having the keys to the kingdom of market movements.

1. The Foundation: Default-Free Interest Rates
The default-free interest rate is the most basic rate of return in an economy. It's the theoretical return you'd get on an investment with absolutely zero risk of not being paid back. In the real world, the closest thing we have to this are government bonds issued by stable, powerful governments, like U.S. Treasury bonds. Investors see these as virtually guaranteed to be repaid.

This rate is the fundamental building block for all other valuations. It sets the "time value of money." When these rates go up, the value of a future dollar goes down. Why? Because you can now earn a higher, guaranteed return elsewhere. So, to be competitive, the price of other assets has to fall to offer a similarly attractive return.

So, how do economic factors pull this lever? The most powerful player here is a country's central bank (like the Federal Reserve in the U.S.).

Inflation: If the central bank sees inflation heating up (the cost of living is rising too fast), it will often raise interest rates. They do this to make borrowing more expensive, which cools down spending and slows the economy, hopefully taming inflation. When this happens, those default-free rates go up across the board. Suddenly, that safe government bond looks more attractive. This forces the prices of riskier assets, like stocks, to come down to compete.

Economic Growth: Conversely, if the economy is sluggish or in a recession, the central bank will likely cut interest rates. This makes it cheaper for businesses to borrow and invest and for consumers to spend, stimulating economic activity. Lower default-free rates make the future cash flows from other investments more valuable in today's terms, which tends to push up their market prices.

Think of the default-free rate as the gravitational pull of the financial system. When it's strong (high rates), it pulls asset values down. When it's weak (low rates), it allows asset values to float higher. Any economic news that hints at what the central bank might do next—an employment report, an inflation reading—will immediately get filtered through this lens and affect market values.

2. The Engine: Expected Cash Flows

This is perhaps the most intuitive lever. The value of a company is directly tied to the profits—or cash flows—it's expected to generate for its owners. Anything that changes the outlook for those future profits will change the company's market value. This applies to the entire market as well; the value of a stock market index, like the S&P 500, is tied to the collective expected profits of all 500 companies within it.

Economic factors are constantly tweaking these expectations.

Economic Cycles: During an economic expansion, people have jobs, they feel confident, and they spend more money. This means higher revenues and profits for most companies. Analysts will revise their forecasts for future cash flows upward, and stock prices will tend to rise. During a recession, the opposite happens. People lose jobs, cut back on spending, and corporate profits shrink. Expected cash flows are revised downward, and market values fall.

Technological Innovation: The invention of the smartphone was a massive economic event. For companies like Apple and Google, it created an unimaginably large new stream of future cash flows, sending their market values soaring. At the same time, it was a death knell for companies that made flip phones or standalone GPS devices. The technology fundamentally altered the timing and magnitude of their expected cash flows—in opposite directions.

Government Regulations and Taxes: A government decision to offer tax credits for electric vehicles directly increases the expected future cash flows for EV manufacturers. A new regulation that increases the cost of compliance for oil and gas companies will decrease their expected cash flows. These policy changes create clear winners and losers, and the market adjusts their values accordingly.

Essentially, any economic news that tells a new story about the future profitability of businesses—a trade deal, a demographic shift, a change in consumer tastes—will directly pull this lever.

3. The Wildcard: The Risk Premium

The final lever is the risk premium. This one is a bit more psychological. The risk premium is the extra return investors demand to compensate them for taking on risk. A safe government bond might pay you 3%, but you're not going to buy a risky stock unless you expect to earn significantly more, maybe 8% or 10%. That extra 5-7% is your risk premium. It's your reward for bearing the uncertainty that the company's cash flows might not materialize as you hope.

This premium isn't static; it expands and contracts based on fear and greed, on uncertainty and confidence.

Geopolitical Events & Uncertainty: When there's a major war, a terrorist attack, or a looming financial crisis, uncertainty skyrockets. Investors become more risk-averse. They aren't willing to take chances unless they are paid handsomely for it. The risk premium they demand goes way up. Even if their expectations for default-free rates and cash flows haven't changed, they will sell off risky assets (stocks) and flock to safer assets (government bonds) until the prices of the risky assets fall enough to offer that higher potential return. This is often called a "flight to safety."

Market Sentiment: Sometimes, the mood of the market itself can change the risk premium. In a bull market, when everyone is optimistic and prices are rising, investors can become complacent. They might demand a smaller risk premium because they perceive the world as less risky. This can push prices up even further. In a bear market, fear takes over, risk premiums expand, and prices fall as investors demand more compensation for any given level of risk.

Economic data that signals instability—like a sudden spike in unemployment or the collapse of a large bank—acts as a catalyst for fear, causing risk premiums to widen and market values to fall, often very quickly.

In summary, every piece of economic news, every data point, and every event is processed by the market through these three channels. It's a constant, dynamic process. A news headline doesn't just "make the market go up." It does so because it caused investors, collectively, to lower their required return (by lowering the risk-free rate or the risk premium) or to raise their expectations for future cash flows. Understanding these three levers gives you a powerful framework for deciphering the seemingly chaotic movements of the market.

The Power of a Story: How Expectations Drive Markets
If the three levers—interest rates, cash flows, and risk premiums—are the machinery of market valuation, then expectations are the fuel that makes the entire engine run. Markets don't react to what is happening right now; they react to what people think will happen in the future. The current price of a stock, bond, or any other asset is nothing more than the collective guess of millions of investors about the future, all rolled into a single number.

This is a profound and crucial concept. It means that the market is always living in the future. The present is already old news. The a company's great earnings report from last quarter is already "priced in." The fact that the economy is currently strong is already reflected in today's asset values. The real action, the real driver of price changes, isn't about what is, but about how our beliefs about what will be are changing.

The Formation of an Expectation

Where do these all-important expectations come from? They are a rich tapestry woven from countless threads of information and analysis.

Hard Data: Investors are constantly sifting through economic reports. Inflation data (like the Consumer Price Index), employment numbers, manufacturing surveys, and GDP growth figures are all pieces of the puzzle. Analysts pore over corporate financial statements—income statements, balance sheets—to project future earnings.

Qualitative Factors: It's not just about numbers. Expectations are also shaped by the "story" of a company or an economy. Is the company's management team visionary and trustworthy? Is a new technology a genuine game-changer or just hype? Is the political climate stable or is there a risk of disruptive policy changes?

Market Sentiment (The Herd): Humans are social creatures, and investors are no exception. The general mood of the market—whether it's wild optimism or deep pessimism—can become a self-fulfilling prophecy. When everyone expects prices to go up, their buying pushes prices up. This psychological component, sometimes called "animal spirits," can cause expectations to detach from underlying fundamentals, at least for a while.

All of this information is synthesized by millions of different people, each with their own biases, analytical methods, and risk tolerances. The resulting market price is the equilibrium point—the price at which buyers and sellers, with all their different expectations, are willing to make a trade.

The Real Mover: Changes in Expectations

This leads us to the most critical point: it is not the news itself, but the surprise in the news that moves markets.

Let's walk through a scenario. Imagine a technology company, "Innovate Corp.," is expected to announce earnings of $1.00 per share. Everyone—from Wall Street analysts to amateur investors—has crunched the numbers, and the consensus is $1.00. The current stock price of Innovate Corp. already reflects this expectation. The market has "priced in" a profit of $1.00 per share.

Now, let's consider three possible outcomes on earnings day:

Innovate Corp. reports earnings of exactly $1.00 per share. What happens to the stock price? Most likely, not much. The company did exactly what everyone expected. The news simply confirms the existing expectation. It's a non-event from the market's perspective.

Innovate Corp. reports a stunning profit of $1.20 per share. This is a positive surprise! The new information forces everyone to change their expectations. They now realize the company is more profitable than they thought. Their models for future cash flows were too low. They will rapidly revise their expectations for the future upward, and this new, more optimistic story will cause a rush of buying. The stock price will likely jump significantly as it adjusts to incorporate this new, better-than-expected reality.

Innovate Corp. reports earnings of $0.80 per share. This is a negative surprise. The company underperformed. The news shatters the old expectation. Investors are now forced to ask tough questions. Was this a one-time problem, or is the company's business model weaker than we believed? They will revise their expectations for future cash flows downward. Fear and uncertainty might also creep in, causing the risk premium they demand to rise. This double-whammy of lower expected cash flows and a higher risk premium will lead to selling, and the stock price will fall.

This dynamic applies to everything. If the market expects the central bank to keep interest rates steady and it suddenly announces a rate hike, markets will be shocked and will have to re-price everything based on this new expectation. If everyone expects a peace treaty to be signed and instead a new conflict breaks out, the expectation of stability is shattered, risk premiums will soar, and markets will fall.

The entire game of investing, in many ways, is about trying to form expectations that are more accurate than the market's collective expectation. It's about anticipating the surprises. Professional investors spend their entire careers trying to find information or develop insights that will allow them to see where the consensus expectation is wrong.

Ultimately, the market is a giant, forward-looking expectations machine. It grinds through millions of data points every second, constantly updating its story about the future. Prices fluctuate not because the world is changing, but because our collective perception of how the world will change is in a constant state of flux. Every price movement you see is simply the market rewriting its story in real-time based on the latest plot twist. Understanding this separates casual observers from savvy participants; it's the realization that in the markets, the future is the only thing that's ever for sale.

The Economic Trio: Growth, Volatility, and Interest Rates

Imagine an economy as a powerful engine. Its performance isn't just about how fast it can go, but also how smoothly it runs and how much it costs to fuel it. This is the essence of the relationship between a country's long-term growth rate, the volatility of that growth, and the average level of real short-term interest rates. They are not three separate issues but three deeply interconnected dials on an economy's dashboard.

The Engine's Speed: Long-Term Growth and the Price of Money

The long-term growth rate is the sustainable speed at which an economy can expand its output of goods and services over many years, after smoothing out the bumps of short-term business cycles. This potential is dictated by fundamental factors like technological innovation, the size and skill of the workforce, and the amount of capital (machinery, infrastructure, etc.) available. A country with a high potential growth rate is like a fertile field promising a bountiful harvest year after year.

This potential directly influences the real interest rate, which is the interest rate after accounting for inflation. Think of the real interest rate as the true cost of borrowing or the true reward for saving. When an economy has many promising opportunities for growth—new factories to build, new technologies to develop, new markets to enter—businesses are eager to borrow money to fund these ventures. This high demand for capital naturally pushes up its price, which is the real interest rate. In essence, a faster-growing economy can support and, in fact, requires higher real interest rates to balance the strong demand for investment with the available supply of savings.

Conversely, an economy with sluggish long-term growth prospects, perhaps due to an aging population or a lack of innovation, will have fewer profitable investment projects. The demand for capital will be weak, leading to lower average real interest rates. There's simply less competition for the available pool of savings. Therefore, the long-term growth rate sets the fundamental, underlying "natural" level for real interest rates.

The Ride's Smoothness: How Volatility Adds a Risk Premium
Now, let's consider the smoothness of the ride, which is the volatility of the growth rate. Two countries might have the same average long-term growth rate of, say, 3%, but they can be vastly different places to invest. One might grow steadily at 3% every year. The other might lurch between booming at 8% one year and crashing to -2% the next, only to average out to 3% over time. This second economy is highly volatile.

Volatility is just another word for risk. Economic and financial uncertainty makes everyone nervous. Lenders become much more cautious. They worry that a sudden downturn could cause borrowers to default on their loans. To compensate for this elevated risk, they demand a higher reward. This "reward for risk" is called a risk premium, and it gets added on top of the natural interest rate. So, an economy with high volatility will almost always have higher average real interest rates than a stable economy with the same growth potential. It's like an insurance company charging a higher premium to a driver with a history of accidents; the underlying risk requires a higher price.

This creates a complex dynamic. On one hand, the uncertainty from volatility might make households and businesses want to save more as a precaution (the "precautionary savings" motive), which would normally push rates down. However, the risk premium demanded by lenders is usually a much stronger force, pushing the overall average rate higher. A stable, predictable economic environment is a valuable asset that allows an economy to function with lower borrowing costs, encouraging more consistent and long-term investment. An unstable, volatile economy pays a constant penalty in the form of higher interest rates, which can act as a drag on the very investment it needs to become more stable.

Riding the Wave: The Business Cycle's Influence on Finance

The economy doesn't grow in a straight line; it breathes in and out in a rhythm known as the business cycle. This cycle has four distinct phases: expansion (growth), peak (the top), contraction (recession), and trough (the bottom). Understanding where we are in this cycle is crucial because it profoundly affects the decisions of central banks, the behavior of interest rates, and the performance of your investments, especially bonds.

Policy and Rates: The Central Bank's Dance with the Cycle

Central banks, like the Federal Reserve in the U.S., act as the economy's chaperones. Their primary job is to maintain stable prices (control inflation) and support maximum employment. They use their main tool, the short-term interest rate, to guide the economy through the business cycle.

During an expansion, the party is in full swing. Businesses are hiring, consumers are spending, and the economy is growing robustly. If this growth becomes too fast, it can lead to overheating, where demand outstrips supply, causing prices to rise rapidly (inflation). To cool things down and prevent inflation from getting out of control, the central bank will step in and raise short-term interest rates.

Higher rates make it more expensive for people to get mortgages and for businesses to get loans for new projects. This dampens spending and investment, slowing the economy to a more sustainable pace.

Conversely, during a contraction or recession, the economy is struggling. People are losing jobs, businesses are failing, and fear is widespread. The central bank's goal is now to stimulate activity and get the economy growing again. To do this, they will aggressively cut short-term interest rates. Cheaper borrowing costs are meant to be an incentive, encouraging households to spend and businesses to invest and hire, effectively jump-starting the economic engine.

The Shape of Things to Come: The Yield Curve
The business cycle doesn't just affect short-term rates; it dramatically alters the entire term structure of interest rates, also known as the yield curve. The yield curve is a snapshot that plots the interest rates (yields) of bonds with equal credit quality but different maturity dates. Its slope is a powerful indicator of market sentiment about the future.

Early Expansion: Right after a recession, the central bank is holding short-term rates very low to stimulate growth. However, investors are looking ahead and see recovery, future growth, and potentially inflation on the horizon. They demand much higher yields to lend their money for long periods (e.g., 10 or 30 years). This combination of very low short-term rates and high long-term rates creates a steeply sloped yield curve. It's a sign of optimism.

Late Expansion: As the expansion matures, the story changes. The central bank has been steadily raising short-term rates to combat inflation, pushing the front end of the curve up. At the same time, investors start to worry that these high rates will eventually choke off growth and lead to a future slowdown. This concern lowers their expectations for future inflation and growth, putting downward pressure on long-term yields. The gap between short and long rates narrows, leading to a flattening yield curve.

Impending Recession: In some cases, the central bank raises short-term rates so much that they actually become higher than long-term rates. This is a rare and ominous sign called an inverted yield curve. It's the market screaming that the central bank's policy is too tight and will inevitably cause a recession, forcing them to slash rates dramatically in the future. It is one of the most reliable predictors of an upcoming economic contraction.

Bond Performance: Timing is Everything

For bond investors, the business cycle is the script for their entire play. The key principle is the inverse relationship between interest rates and bond prices: when interest rates fall, prices of existing bonds rise, and when interest rates rise, bond prices fall. Furthermore, longer-maturity bonds are much more sensitive to these changes than short-maturity bonds.

Knowing this, we can see how bonds perform in different phases:

During a Contraction/Recession: This is the best time to own bonds, especially long-maturity bonds. As the central bank cuts interest rates to stimulate the economy, all bond prices will rise. But because long-term bonds are the most sensitive, they experience the largest price gains, delivering handsome returns to investors.

During an Expansion: This is a difficult environment for bondholders. The central bank is raising interest rates to prevent overheating. As rates climb, the prices of existing bonds fall. Long-maturity bonds perform the worst during this period, as their prices suffer the biggest drops. Investors often prefer shorter-term bonds or other assets during this phase.

By understanding the rhythm of the business cycle, you can better anticipate the actions of the central bank and position your bond investments to either benefit from falling rates or protect yourself from rising ones.

The Dance Between Certainty and Surprise: Unpacking Yield Spreads

Imagine you have two bonds. One is a regular, old-school bond—we'll call it a nominal bond. It promises to pay you a fixed interest rate, say 4%, no matter what. The other is a bit fancier; it's an inflation-indexed bond, often called a TIPS (Treasury Inflation-Protected Security) in the United States. This bond is clever. It promises a lower fixed rate, maybe 1%, but it also adjusts its value based on inflation. So, if inflation goes up, the bond's value and its interest payments also increase to protect your purchasing power. The difference in the yields between these two types of bonds is called the yield spread, or more specifically, the breakeven inflation rate. This spread isn't just a random number; it's a fascinating story told by the market about its feelings, fears, and expectations. Let's explore the main characters in this story.

The Star of the Show: Expected Inflation

The most significant factor influencing this spread is, without a doubt, expected inflation. Think of the yield on the nominal bond as having two main parts: the "real" return (what you're actually earning after accounting for inflation) and the market's best guess about future inflation. The inflation-indexed bond, on the other hand, explicitly separates these. Its yield is the real return because the inflation part is adjusted for automatically.

So, the spread between them becomes the market's collective forecast for inflation. If the 10-year nominal Treasury bond yields 4% and the 10-year TIPS yields 1.5%, the spread is 2.5%. This 2.5% is the breakeven inflation rate. It means that investors are, on average, expecting inflation to be around 2.5% per year for the next decade. If actual inflation turns out to be higher than 2.5%, the TIPS investor wins because their bond will adjust upward more than expected. If inflation is lower than 2.5%, the nominal bond investor comes out ahead because their fixed 4% return is eroded less than anticipated. Central banks and economists watch this number like a hawk because it provides a real-time pulse of what everyone—from giant pension funds to individual savers—thinks about future prices. It's a powerful, crowd-sourced economic indicator.

The Mysterious Co-Star: The Inflation Risk Premium
But wait, there's a twist. The spread isn't just about expected inflation. There's another, more subtle character at play: the inflation risk premium. Investing is all about dealing with uncertainty, and inflation is one of the biggest uncertainties out there. What if the experts are wrong? What if a sudden geopolitical event or a supply chain shock sends inflation soaring unexpectedly?

Holding a nominal bond is like making a bet that inflation will behave. If you're wrong and inflation spikes, the fixed payments you receive will be worth much less in the real world. You'll be able to buy fewer groceries, less gas, and smaller coffees with your coupon payments. To compensate for this risk—the risk that inflation could be a wild card—investors demand a little extra yield on nominal bonds. This extra bit of compensation is the inflation risk premium.

This premium can be positive or negative, though it's usually positive. When people are very nervous about the future and feel inflation is unpredictable, this premium gets bigger. The nominal bond has to offer an even juicier yield to lure investors away from the safety of the inflation-indexed bond. Conversely, in calm, stable economic times when everyone feels confident that the central bank has inflation under control, this risk premium might shrink or even disappear. This premium is a "squishy" number, hard to pin down exactly, but it's a crucial part of the yield spread story, reflecting the market's collective anxiety level.

The Supporting Cast: Liquidity and Technical Factors
Finally, we have the supporting cast, which includes liquidity. Liquidity is just a fancy word for how easily you can buy or sell something without affecting its price. The market for regular, nominal Treasury bonds is enormous and incredibly liquid. It's like a massive, bustling superhighway where trades happen instantly. The market for inflation-indexed bonds, while substantial, is smaller and a bit less traveled—more like a major city road.

Because of this difference, investors might demand a small premium to hold the less liquid asset. This is called a liquidity premium. In normal times, this effect is pretty small. But during a crisis, it can become a huge deal. When panic hits the markets, everyone rushes for the exits, and they all want to sell their assets for the most liquid thing available: cash or, the next best thing, nominal Treasury bonds. This "flight to quality" can cause the demand for nominal bonds to surge, pushing their yields down, while demand for less liquid inflation-indexed bonds might fall, pushing their yields up. This can make the spread between them do strange things that have little to do with long-term inflation expectations and everything to do with short-term fear. This technical factor can temporarily distort the beautiful, clean story told by the breakeven inflation rate, reminding us that markets are not just driven by cold, hard numbers, but also by human emotion.

Riding the Economic Rollercoaster: Credit Spreads and the Business Cycle

Now, let's switch gears and talk about the world of corporate bonds. Unlike government bonds, which are generally considered risk-free (especially those from stable governments like the U.S.), corporate bonds carry credit risk. This is the risk that the company issuing the bond might run into financial trouble and fail to make its promised interest payments or repay the principal. To convince investors to take on this extra risk, companies have to offer a higher yield than the government. The difference between a corporate bond's yield and a comparable government bond's yield is called the credit spread.

This spread is the market's price for taking on default risk. A wide spread means investors are very worried and demand a lot of compensation. A narrow or "tight" spread means investors feel confident and are willing to accept less compensation for the risk. This spread is not static; it breathes in and out with the rhythm of the economy, widening and tightening as we move through the four phases of the business cycle: expansion, peak, contraction (recession), and trough.

Sunny Skies and Tight Spreads: The Expansion Phase

During an economic expansion, the world looks bright. Companies are making money hand over fist, profits are growing, and jobs are plentiful. People are spending, businesses are investing, and the future seems full of promise. In this happy environment, the risk of a company going bankrupt seems very low.

As a result, investors become more optimistic and have a greater appetite for risk. They look at the extra yield offered by corporate bonds and think, "That's a great deal!" They are less worried about defaults, so they don't demand a huge premium for taking on credit risk. This high demand for corporate bonds pushes their prices up and their yields down. Since government bond yields might also be rising slightly as the central bank tries to keep the booming economy from overheating, the gap between the two—the credit spread—narrows or tightens.

For investors holding credit-sensitive bonds (like high-yield or "junk" bonds), this is the best of times. Not only are they collecting their regular coupon payments, but the value of their bonds is also increasing as spreads tighten. It's a period of strong performance for anyone holding corporate debt. The economic sun is shining, and credit spreads are basking in its warmth.

Dark Clouds Gathering: The Contraction Phase

Eventually, the party ends. The economy reaches its peak and begins to slow down, entering a contraction or recession. 😨 Corporate profits start to shrink, companies lay off workers, and consumers cut back on spending. The future suddenly looks much more uncertain and scary.

In this environment of fear and pessimism, investors' attitudes do a complete 180. The possibility of companies defaulting on their debt is no longer a distant thought; it's a very real and present danger. Investors flee from risk, selling their corporate bonds and rushing to the safety of government bonds. This is that same "flight to quality" we mentioned earlier.

This mass sell-off of corporate bonds causes their prices to plummet and their yields to skyrocket. Meanwhile, the surge in demand for government bonds pushes their yields down. The combined effect is a dramatic widening of the credit spread. A spread that was once narrow and tight now balloons, reflecting the market's immense fear of corporate defaults.

For investors holding credit-sensitive instruments, this phase is brutal. The value of their portfolios can fall sharply as spreads blow out. The higher yields might look tempting, but they come with the very real risk that the company could go under, wiping out the entire investment. This is when the true risk of credit-sensitive bonds becomes painfully clear. The performance of these instruments suffers greatly during recessions as investors prioritize the return of their money over the return on their money. The cycle, from trough to expansion and back again, shows how deeply the fate of corporate debt is tied to the health of the overall economy.

How a Company's Product Markets Affect Its Credit Quality

Think of a company's credit quality as its financial trustworthiness. When lenders, like banks or bond investors, decide whether to lend a company money, they are essentially asking one big question: "How likely is this company to pay us back, on time and in full?" A company with high credit quality is seen as a very reliable borrower, while one with low credit quality is considered risky. The answer to this question isn't just found on a balance sheet; it's deeply rooted in the real world—specifically, in the markets where the company sells its products or services.

The characteristics of these markets can either build a fortress around a company's finances or leave it exposed to the slightest economic breeze. Let's break down how this works.

The Industry Rollercoaster: Cyclical vs. Non-Cyclical Markets

Imagine two companies. One sells luxury sports cars, and the other sells bread and milk. When the economy is booming and people have plenty of disposable income, the sports car company is likely doing fantastically well. But when a recession hits and people lose their jobs, a $100,000 car is one of the first things to be cut from the budget. This company is in a cyclical industry because its fortunes ride the waves of the broader economic cycle. Its revenues can be incredibly volatile—soaring one year and plummeting the next.

Now think about the company selling bread and milk. Whether the economy is great or terrible, people still need to eat. Sales might dip slightly, but they will remain relatively stable. This company is in a non-cyclical (or defensive) industry.

For a lender, this difference is monumental. A company with highly volatile revenues and cash flows, like the luxury car maker, is a riskier bet. During a downturn, its ability to make debt payments could be seriously jeopardized. The non-cyclical company, with its steady and predictable cash flow, looks far more reliable. It's like lending money to a person with a stable, fixed salary versus someone who works purely on unpredictable commissions. The salaried person will almost always be seen as having higher credit quality. Therefore, companies in non-cyclical industries like consumer staples, utilities, and healthcare generally have stronger credit quality than those in cyclical sectors like automotive, travel, and high-end retail.

The Competitive Arena: Who Has the Power?

The structure of the market a company competes in is another crucial factor. This determines how much power the company has to set prices and protect its profits.

Monopoly or Oligopoly: In a market with very few competitors (an oligopoly) or just one (a monopoly), a company has immense pricing power. Think of your local utility provider for electricity or a major telecommunications company. Because customers have few, if any, alternatives, these companies can maintain stable prices and generate predictable profits. This predictability is music to a lender's ears and translates into very high credit quality.

Perfect Competition: At the other extreme is a market with tons of competitors all selling an identical product. Think of small-scale farmers selling wheat. No single farmer can influence the price; they are "price takers." This environment is brutal. Competition is fierce, profit margins are razor-thin, and a company's financial health can change in an instant. This high level of uncertainty and lack of pricing power leads to lower credit quality.

Most companies fall somewhere in between, in what's called monopolistic competition, where they sell similar but not identical products. This is where the next two factors become so important.

Building a Moat: Barriers to Entry

Barriers to entry are obstacles that make it difficult for new competitors to enter a market. A company protected by high barriers is like a castle surrounded by a deep moat. It can defend its market share and profitability far more easily.

What are these barriers? They can be things like:

High Capital Costs: It takes billions of dollars to build a new semiconductor factory or an automotive plant.

Patents and Intellectual Property: A pharmaceutical company with a patent on a blockbuster drug is protected from competition for years.

Strong Brand Loyalty: Companies like Coca-Cola or Apple have built such powerful brands that it's incredibly difficult for a newcomer to win over their customers.

Government Regulations: Industries like banking or defense are heavily regulated, making it tough for new players to get started.

When a company benefits from high barriers to entry, its future cash flows are more secure. Lenders know that a swarm of new, low-cost competitors isn't going to suddenly appear and destroy the company's profitability. This security leads to higher credit quality. Conversely, a business in an industry with low barriers, like a local coffee shop or a t-shirt printing company, is constantly at risk from new entrants, making it a riskier proposition for lenders.

Standing Out from the Crowd: Product Differentiation
Finally, how unique is the company's product? If a company sells a commodity—something that is basically the same no matter who produces it—it can only compete on price. This often leads to price wars that erode profits for everyone.

However, if a company has successfully differentiated its product, it can escape this trap. Product differentiation means that customers perceive the company's product as unique or superior in some way, whether due to quality, design, brand image, or technology. Apple is a classic example. An iPhone is functionally a smartphone, but its design, ecosystem, and brand allow Apple to charge a significant premium over its competitors.

This ability to command a higher price and foster customer loyalty creates a more resilient revenue stream. Even in a downturn, loyal customers are less likely to switch to a cheaper alternative. This resilience and pricing power directly support stronger, more stable cash flows, which in turn leads to superior credit quality. A company that can't differentiate itself is at the mercy of the market, making its ability to repay debt far less certain.

In essence, a lender looks at a company's markets to tell a story about its future. A company in a stable industry, with few competitors, high barriers to entry, and a unique, desirable product, is telling a story of predictable and durable cash flows. That story is what earns it the label of high credit quality.

The Equity Risk Premium and Hedging Your Lifestyle

The equity risk premium (ERP) is one of the most important ideas in finance. In simple terms, it's the extra return that investors demand to choose a risky investment, like stocks, over a completely safe one, like a government bond. We know stocks have historically provided much higher returns than bonds over the long run, and the ERP is that difference. But why does it exist? Why do stocks have to offer this premium?

The answer lies in a surprisingly human concept: our desire to have a stable life, or what economists call "consumption smoothing." And it turns out, stocks are terrible at helping us do that. This makes them a very poor hedge against the biggest risks in our lives.

Your Financial Umbrella: The Idea of a Consumption Hedge

We all want to maintain a relatively stable standard of living. We want to be able to pay our mortgage, buy groceries, and go on vacation, not just when times are good, but also when times are bad. An asset that helps us achieve this is called a good consumption hedge.

Think of a perfect consumption hedge as a magical insurance policy. It pays you money exactly when you need it the most. Your house fire insurance is a great example. It has a massive payout precisely at the moment your financial world is turned upside down by a fire. It helps you "smooth" your life by providing cash to rebuild when you'd otherwise have nothing. It's your financial umbrella for a very specific type of storm.

Now, let's expand this idea to the biggest financial storm most people face: a recession. During a recession, your personal income is at its greatest risk. You might get laid off, your hours might be cut, or your small business might struggle. This is when you need your investments to come to the rescue. A good consumption hedge would be an asset that increases in value during a recession, giving you cash to spend when your other income has dried up.

Do Stocks Work Like an Umbrella?

So, how do stocks perform as a consumption hedge? Are they the trusty umbrella that will keep you dry during an economic storm?

The answer is a resounding no. In fact, stocks are the complete opposite. They are like an umbrella that not only disappears when it starts to rain but also somehow makes you wetter.

Think about it:

When do stock markets tend to crash? They tend to fall dramatically during recessions and broad economic downturns.

When is your job or business income most at risk? During those very same recessions.

This is the critical connection. Stocks perform poorly precisely at the moment when you, as an investor, are most likely to be struggling financially. Their value goes down just as your income from your job is also going down. Instead of helping you smooth your consumption, they make the bad times even worse. An investment that does well when you're already doing well (a booming economy) and does terribly when you're doing terribly (a recession) is a terrible consumption hedge.

This property is known as having returns that are pro-cyclical. They are positively correlated with the economic cycle and, by extension, with our own financial well-being.

The Price of Bad Insurance: Explaining the Premium

This brings us back to the main question. If stocks are such a lousy hedge against the bad times we all want to avoid, why on earth would any rational person invest in them?

The only reason is that they are "priced" to reflect this massive flaw. Because stocks offer you no comfort or insurance in bad times, they have to offer you something else to make them attractive: the promise of a very high average return over the long run. This is the equity risk premium.

Let's go back to the insurance analogy. Imagine someone tried to sell you a car insurance policy that only covered accidents that happened on empty roads on sunny days. You'd laugh at them, because it fails to protect you when you need it most—in a blizzard or in rush-hour traffic. To entice you to buy such a flawed policy, they would have to offer it to you for an incredibly cheap price.

Stocks are like that flawed insurance policy. They fail you in the "blizzards" of recessions. Therefore, for investors to be willing to hold them, the price of stocks today must be low enough relative to their expected future earnings and dividends to generate a high expected return. That high expected return is the compensation—the premium—you demand for taking on the risk of holding an asset that will kick you when you're already down.

So, the relationship is this: the poorer an asset's consumption hedging properties, the higher the risk premium it must offer. An asset that pays off in bad times (a good hedge) is incredibly valuable and investors will accept a low return to hold it. An asset that gets crushed in bad times (a bad hedge, like stocks) is fundamentally undesirable from a risk-management perspective, and so it must promise a high return to find any buyers.

The equity risk premium isn't just a reward for volatility; it's a reward for holding an asset that magnifies, rather than mitigates, life's biggest financial risks. It's the price we demand for owning an umbrella that we know will vanish at the first sign of rain.

The Business Cycle's Grip on Earnings Expectations

The business cycle is the economy's natural rhythm, its heartbeat of expansion and contraction. This ebb and flow doesn't just affect whether people are getting jobs or buying new cars; it fundamentally shapes how investors and analysts view a company's future profitability. Both short-term and long-term earnings growth expectations are deeply intertwined with where we are in this cycle.

Short-Term Earnings: Riding the Economic Wave

In the expansion phase, the economy is humming. Consumer confidence is high, people are spending, and businesses are investing. This optimistic environment directly fuels short-term earnings expectations. For cyclical companies—those in industries like automotive, luxury goods, and travel—this period is a bonanza. Analysts will project robust quarter-over-quarter and year-over-year earnings growth. They see rising demand and pricing power, allowing companies to boost their profit margins. A car manufacturer, for instance, is expected to sell more vehicles at higher prices when people feel secure in their jobs. These positive forecasts are often self-fulfilling, as high expectations can drive stock prices up, encouraging more investment and spending.

As the economy reaches its peak, the party is in full swing, but the music is about to stop. Short-term expectations are often at their most euphoric right before a downturn. Companies might report record profits, but savvy analysts start looking for cracks. Are input costs rising too fast? Is consumer debt getting too high? While the reported earnings might be fantastic, the expectations for the next quarter might start to temper. The growth rate is expected to slow down, even if the absolute numbers are still good. It's a subtle shift from "things are great" to "things are still good, but maybe not for long."

Then comes the contraction phase, or recession. This is where short-term earnings expectations turn bleak. Layoffs rise, consumer spending plummets, and businesses slash their budgets. Analysts will sharply revise their earnings forecasts downward. Companies that were recently expected to post double-digit growth might now be projected to have flat or even negative growth. During this phase, companies often issue "earnings warnings," signaling to the market that they won't meet their previously optimistic targets. For defensive sectors, like consumer staples (think toothpaste and toilet paper) and utilities, the expectations don't fall as dramatically because demand for their products is relatively stable. People still need to brush their teeth, even in a recession.

Finally, the cycle hits the trough. This is the bottom, the point of maximum pessimism. Short-term earnings expectations are at their lowest. Companies are reporting losses, and analysts are forecasting more of the same. However, it's at this very point that a crucial shift begins. Expectations are so low that they become easy to beat. A company might still report a loss, but if the loss is smaller than anticipated, the market often reacts positively. This is the "less bad is good" phenomenon. It's here that the seeds of the next expansion are sown, as expectations begin to slowly, cautiously, turn positive again.

Long-Term Earnings: Looking Beyond the Horizon 🔭
The business cycle also casts a long shadow over long-term earnings growth expectations, though in a more nuanced way. Long-term forecasts (typically 5-10 years out) try to look past the immediate noise of a recession or a boom and focus on a company's fundamental, sustainable growth potential.

During an expansion, analysts might extrapolate the good times a little too far into the future. They may build models assuming strong economic growth will continue indefinitely, leading to overly optimistic long-term growth rates. This is especially true for "growth" stocks in innovative sectors like technology. The narrative becomes one of unstoppable progress, and the long-term earnings potential is seen as almost limitless. However, a more sober analysis would incorporate the idea of "mean reversion"—the theory that growth rates will eventually revert to the long-term average.

Conversely, during a contraction, pessimism can infect long-term views. When companies are struggling to survive, it's hard to imagine them thriving a decade from now. Analysts might slash their long-term growth assumptions, assuming that the current economic pain will permanently impair a company's ability to innovate, invest, and compete. They might project that a company will lose market share forever or that an entire industry will be structurally smaller. For example, during a deep recession, one might incorrectly assume that people will never travel or dine out with the same frequency again. This can lead to undervaluing high-quality companies that have the resilience to survive the downturn and flourish in the subsequent recovery. The trough of the cycle is often the point of maximum opportunity for long-term investors who can see past the immediate despair and recognize that the cycle will, inevitably, turn.

Ultimately, the smartest analysts and investors understand that the business cycle influences everything. They adjust their long-term models to account for an entire cycle—not just the phase we are in today. They normalize earnings, trying to estimate what a company could earn on average, through both the good times and the bad, to get a clearer picture of its true long-term potential.

How Economic Cycles Inflate and Deflate Valuation Multiples

Valuation multiples, like the famous price-to-earnings (P/E) ratio, are essentially a measure of market sentiment. They tell us how much investors are willing to pay for one dollar of a company's earnings, sales, or book value. These multiples are not static; they breathe in and out with the rhythm of the business cycle, expanding with optimism and contracting with fear.

The Expansion and Peak: Paying a Premium for Sunshine

During an economic expansion, everything looks rosy. Corporate earnings are growing, unemployment is low, and the future seems bright. This widespread optimism directly translates into higher valuation multiples. Why? Several psychological and financial factors are at play.

First, investor confidence is high. When people feel good about the economy and their own financial prospects, they are more willing to take on risk. They bid up stock prices in anticipation of even stronger future earnings. The "E" (Earnings) in the P/E ratio is growing, but the "P" (Price) often grows even faster, causing the whole multiple to expand. Investors are essentially paying a premium for expected growth.

Second, interest rates are often low to moderate at the beginning of an expansion, as central banks try to stimulate the economy. Lower interest rates make stocks more attractive compared to safer assets like bonds. When bonds are yielding very little, investors are pushed into the stock market to seek higher returns, further driving up prices and multiples. This is often referred to as the "TINA" effect: There Is No Alternative to stocks.

As the cycle moves towards its peak, this expansion of multiples can reach euphoric levels. The narrative of endless growth takes hold. Analysts project high earnings growth far into the future, and investors are willing to pay very high multiples (e.g., P/E ratios of 30, 40, or even higher) based on those rosy forecasts. This is when you hear talk of "new paradigms" that supposedly justify the high valuations. However, this is also the point of greatest risk. The high multiple means that expectations are sky-high, and any disappointment can cause a sharp and painful correction.

The Contraction and Trough: A Flight to Safety 🌧️
When the cycle turns and a contraction begins, the mood sours quickly. Uncertainty replaces confidence. The same forces that pushed multiples up now work in reverse to pull them down.

First, fear and risk aversion take over. As earnings decline and companies start announcing layoffs, investors panic. They sell stocks and flee to the safety of cash or government bonds. This selling pressure drives down the "P" in the P/E ratio. Even if a company manages to maintain its earnings, its stock price will likely fall as investors demand a lower multiple to compensate them for the higher perceived risk. The entire market gets de-rated.

Second, the earnings picture becomes murky. During a recession, the "E" in the P/E ratio is not only falling but is also highly unpredictable. How bad will it get? How long will it last? This uncertainty makes investors unwilling to pay a high price for those uncertain future earnings. They would rather wait for clarity. In some cases, the "E" can even turn negative (a loss), making the P/E ratio meaningless. Other multiples, like price-to-book or price-to-sales, become more relevant, but they too will contract as investor sentiment worsens.

At the trough of the cycle, multiples are typically at their lowest. Pessimism is rampant. No one wants to own stocks. P/E ratios for the overall market can fall into the single digits. It's at this point that stocks are often at their cheapest, offering the greatest potential for future returns. For a value investor, the trough is a shopping paradise. They can buy shares in good companies at a significant discount, knowing that as the economy inevitably recovers, both the earnings and the multiple applied to those earnings will rise, providing a powerful double boost to the stock price. The cycle shows us that the price you pay for earnings is just as important as the earnings themselves, and that price is heavily influenced by the collective mood of the market.

Economic Forces Shaping Commercial Real Estate Investment

Commercial real estate (CRE)—think office buildings, shopping malls, warehouses, and apartment complexes—is a foundational part of the economy. But as an investment, it's incredibly sensitive to the economic currents swirling around it. Investors in this space must be part economist, part forecaster, because a handful of key economic factors can make or break their returns.

The Big Picture: GDP and Employment Growth

At the most fundamental level, the demand for commercial real estate is a direct function of economic growth, measured by Gross Domestic Product (GDP). When the economy is expanding, businesses are growing. They need more office space to house their employees, more warehouse space to store and distribute their goods, and more retail space to sell their products. This drives up demand for properties, leading to higher occupancy rates and allowing landlords to charge higher rents. Higher rents, in turn, increase the property's income and its overall value. A rising GDP is the tide that lifts all CRE boats.

Closely linked to GDP is the employment rate. More jobs mean more people needing a place to work. A city with a booming tech or finance sector will see soaring demand for office space. Similarly, a region with a growing manufacturing base will need more industrial and warehouse facilities. Employment growth also puts more money into people's pockets, which boosts consumer spending and supports retail properties like shopping centers. Furthermore, job growth attracts people to an area, increasing the demand for apartments and multifamily housing. Conversely, when unemployment rises during a recession, businesses downsize, office vacancies spike, and retail stores close, sending shockwaves through the CRE market.

The Cost of Money: Interest Rates and Capital Availability 💰

Commercial real estate is a capital-intensive business. Very few investors buy a skyscraper with cash. They rely on debt, and the cost of that debt is determined by interest rates. When interest rates are low, borrowing is cheap. This makes it easier and more profitable for developers to get loans for new construction projects and for investors to finance acquisitions. Lower rates also mean that the required return, or "cap rate," that investors demand from a property can be lower. This pushes property values up.

The reverse is true when interest rates rise. Higher borrowing costs can halt new development projects in their tracks and make it harder for buyers to secure financing. This reduces demand for properties. More importantly, as the yield on safer investments like government bonds goes up, real estate becomes relatively less attractive. Investors will demand a higher return (a higher cap rate) to compensate them for the risk, which puts downward pressure on property values. The availability of capital from banks and other lenders is also crucial. In a credit crunch, even if rates are low, lenders might be unwilling to extend loans, effectively freezing the market.

Inflation and Demographics: The Slow-Burn Factors 🔥

Inflation, the rate at which the general level of prices for goods and services is rising, has a complex relationship with CRE. On one hand, real estate is often seen as a good hedge against inflation. As the cost of living goes up, landlords can often increase rents, especially if their leases are tied to an inflation index. This protects the real value of their income stream. The cost to build a new building also rises with inflation, which can make existing properties more valuable by comparison. However, high inflation often forces central banks to raise interest rates aggressively, which, as we've seen, is a major headwind for property values.

Finally, long-term demographic and social trends are powerful, slow-moving forces. An aging population might increase demand for healthcare facilities and senior housing. The rise of e-commerce has created an unprecedented boom in demand for modern logistics warehouses while simultaneously devastating traditional shopping malls. The recent shift towards remote and hybrid work is fundamentally reshaping the demand for office space in major city centers. Investors who can correctly anticipate these deep-seated trends—like population migration to sunbelt states or the demand for sustainable, green buildings—can position themselves for outsized returns, regardless of the short-term gyrations of the business cycle.

Analysis of Active Portfolio Management

Unpacking the Value of Active Management and Key Performance Ratios

Investing can sometimes feel like navigating a vast ocean. You can choose to simply drift with the current by investing in a passive index fund, which mirrors a market benchmark like the S&P 500. This is a perfectly fine strategy for many. Or, you can hire a skilled captain—an active portfolio manager—who promises to navigate the seas, dodge the storms, and find treasure-laden islands that others miss, aiming to deliver a return better than the general market tide.

But how do you know if your captain is truly a skilled navigator or just lucky? How can you measure the extra value, or "alpha," they claim to provide? This is where specific tools and metrics become crucial. We're going to dive deep into how to measure the value an active manager adds and then explore two of the most important tools for this job: the Information Ratio and the Sharpe Ratio.

Part 1: How is the Value Added by Active Management Measured?

When an active manager takes the helm of your portfolio, their primary promise is to outperform a specific benchmark. If their chosen universe is large U.S. stocks, their benchmark might be the S&P 500. If they invest in international tech companies, the benchmark will be a relevant global technology index. Simply beating the benchmark isn't enough, though. A manager could take on massive, stomach-churning risks to achieve that outperformance. If your portfolio value swings wildly day to day, the stress might not be worth the extra return.

The true value added by active management is the risk-adjusted outperformance. We need to see if the manager generated returns superior to the benchmark after accounting for the level of risk they took. It's about skill, not just brute force. Here's how we measure it.

The Concept of "Alpha"

At the heart of measuring active management is the concept of alpha. Think of alpha as the secret sauce. It's the portion of a portfolio's return that can't be explained by the general movement of the market. It is, in theory, the direct result of the manager's unique skill in picking the right investments at the right time. A positive alpha means the manager added value; a negative alpha means they destroyed it, and you would have been better off just owning the benchmark.

Imagine the benchmark returned 10% in a year. Your actively managed fund returned 12%. On the surface, it looks like the manager added 2% of value. But what if they took on 50% more risk than the benchmark to get there? Was it worth it? Alpha helps us answer this.

Jensen's Alpha: A Classic Measure

One of the most common ways to quantify this is through Jensen's Alpha. This metric, developed by economist Michael Jensen, elegantly calculates the excess return of a portfolio over its expected return, given its level of risk.

The expected return is calculated using the Capital Asset Pricing Model (CAPM). Don't let the name intimidate you. The CAPM is just a formula that sets a baseline for what a portfolio should have earned. It considers three things:

The Risk-Free Rate: The return you could get on a virtually risk-free investment, like a U.S. Treasury bill.

The Benchmark Return: The performance of the market or benchmark index.

Beta: This is a crucial piece. Beta measures the portfolio's volatility or sensitivity relative to the benchmark. A beta of 1.0 means the portfolio moves in lockstep with the market. A beta of 1.2 means it's 20% more volatile (it goes up more when the market is up, and down more when the market is down). A beta of 0.8 means it's 20% less volatile.

The CAPM formula gives you the return you should expect for taking on a certain amount of market risk (beta). Jensen's Alpha is then the difference between what the fund actually earned and what it was expected to earn.

Formula for Jensen's Alpha:
Alpha = Portfolio's Actual Return – [Risk-Free Rate + Beta × (Benchmark Return – Risk-Free Rate)]

Let's use an example:

Portfolio's Actual Return: 15%

Risk-Free Rate: 2%

Benchmark (S&P 500) Return: 12%

Portfolio's Beta: 1.1

First, we calculate the expected return using CAPM:
Expected Return = 2% + 1.1 × (12% – 2%) = 2% + 1.1 × (10%) = 2% + 11% = 13%

Now, we find the alpha:
Jensen's Alpha = 15% (Actual Return) – 13% (Expected Return) = +2%

This positive alpha of 2% indicates that the manager delivered returns that were 2 percentage points higher than what would be expected for the amount of market risk they took on. This is a direct measure of their value-add. If the alpha were negative, it would signal that the manager underperformed on a risk-adjusted basis, even if their raw return beat the benchmark. It suggests their security selection or market timing was poor, and investors were not adequately compensated for the risk.

Measuring value is therefore a nuanced process. It's about peeling back the layers of raw performance to see if the engine driving it is genuine skill (positive alpha) or just a willingness to take on excessive risk.

Part 2: The Information Ratio vs. The Sharpe Ratio
Once we've established that a manager is generating alpha, we want to know how consistently they do it. A manager who delivers a huge alpha one year but then massively underperforms for the next two isn't very reliable. This is where the Information Ratio shines. To understand its unique role, it's best to contrast it with the more widely known Sharpe Ratio.

These two ratios are like two different diagnostic tools for a doctor. Both measure health (risk-adjusted returns), but they look at different aspects and answer different questions.

The Sharpe Ratio: A Measure of Overall Performance
The Sharpe Ratio, developed by Nobel laureate William F. Sharpe, is arguably the most famous measure of risk-adjusted return. It answers the question: "For every unit of total risk I took, how much excess return did I get?"

It's a broad, high-level view. It doesn't care where the return comes from—whether it's from simply being in the market or from a manager's skill. It also doesn't care about a benchmark. It simply looks at the portfolio's return, subtracts the risk-free rate, and divides it by the portfolio's total volatility (measured by standard deviation).

Formula for the Sharpe Ratio:
Sharpe Ratio = (Portfolio's Return – Risk-Free Rate) / Portfolio's Standard Deviation

A higher Sharpe Ratio is better. It means the investment is giving you more bang for your buck in terms of return for the amount of volatility you have to endure. It's a great tool for comparing completely different investment strategies (e.g., a real estate fund vs. a tech stock fund) because it puts them on a level playing field of risk and return.

The Information Ratio: A Measure of Manager Skill and Consistency
The Information Ratio (IR) is a much more specialized tool. It's designed specifically to evaluate an active manager's performance against their benchmark. It answers a very different question: "How consistently can my manager generate excess returns over the benchmark, relative to the volatility of those excess returns?"

The IR drills down into the manager's alpha. It focuses only on the performance that is different from the benchmark.

Formula for the Information Ratio:
Information Ratio = (Portfolio's Return – Benchmark's Return) / Tracking Error

Let's break down its components:

Active Return (the numerator): This is simply the portfolio's return minus the benchmark's return. It's the "alpha" we discussed, but in its raw form before other risk adjustments.

Tracking Error (the denominator): This is the key. Tracking error measures how much the portfolio's returns deviate from the benchmark's returns over time. It is the standard deviation of the active return. A high tracking error means the manager is taking big bets that are very different from the benchmark, leading to performance that can swing wildly above or below it. A low tracking error means the manager stays pretty close to the benchmark's composition.

A high Information Ratio is the holy grail for active management. It indicates that the manager produces a high level of excess return on a very consistent basis (low tracking error). An IR of 0.5 is considered good, while an IR of 1.0 or higher is exceptional and very rare to sustain.

Ex Post vs. Ex Ante Information Ratio
The Information Ratio can be viewed in two ways:

Ex Post (Historical): This is the IR calculated using past performance data. You look at the historical returns of the portfolio and the benchmark to compute the active return and tracking error. It tells you how skilled the manager was. It's a report card on their past performance.

Ex Ante (Forward-Looking): This is a forecasted IR. Analysts build models to predict a manager's expected alpha and their expected tracking error. This is much more of an art than a science, as it relies on assumptions about the manager's skill, the market environment, and how much freedom they have to deviate from the benchmark. The ex-ante IR is used to decide whether to hire a manager in the first place. It's a prediction of how skilled they will be.

Imagine you have two managers. Manager A has a higher Sharpe Ratio, but Manager B has a higher Information Ratio. What does this mean?

It likely means that Manager A is delivering a better overall return for the total risk taken, perhaps by having exposure to factors that did well but are not part of the benchmark. Their total portfolio is very efficient. Manager B, however, is a master at their specific game. They are exceptionally good and consistent at beating their specific benchmark. If your goal is to find someone to beat the S&P 500 with reliable skill, Manager B and their high Information Ratio is likely your choice. If you just want the best risk-adjusted return possible, regardless of a benchmark, Manager A's high Sharpe Ratio is more compelling.

In conclusion, measuring the value of active management requires looking beyond simple returns. By using tools like Jensen's Alpha, we can identify a manager's true skill. And by using the Information Ratio alongside the Sharpe Ratio, we can gain a complete picture of not only a portfolio's overall efficiency but also the consistency and reliability of the manager hired to beat the market.

The Heart of the Hunt: Deconstructing the Fundamental Law of Active Portfolio Management

Imagine you're the owner of a sports team, and you want to win the championship. Winning isn't about luck; it's about having a strategy that consistently puts you in a better position than your opponents. In the world of investing, this strategic edge is what active portfolio management is all about. The Fundamental Law of Active Portfolio Management is like the master playbook for this game. It's a simple yet incredibly powerful formula that breaks down exactly where a manager's success comes from.

The law essentially states that a manager's risk-adjusted active return, known as the Information Ratio (IR), is determined by their skill and how effectively they can apply that skill across many opportunities.

This might seem a bit technical, but let's break down each piece of this puzzle. Think of it as a recipe for investment success. Each component is a crucial ingredient, and understanding them reveals whether a manager is a master chef or just a lucky cook.

Information Coefficient (IC): The Skill Ingredient 🧠
The Information Coefficient (IC) is the absolute core of the law. It measures a manager's raw forecasting skill. Plain and simple, it answers the question: "When you make a prediction, how often are you right?"

The IC is a correlation score that ranges from -1.0 to +1.0.

An IC of +1.0 is perfection. Every single forecast you make comes true. If you predict a stock will go up, it goes up. If you predict it will go down, it goes down. This is the holy grail, and in reality, it's impossible to achieve.

An IC of 0 means there is absolutely no relationship between your forecasts and what actually happens. Your picks are no better than random chance—like flipping a coin to decide whether to buy or sell.

An IC of -1.0 means you are perfectly wrong, every single time. While this sounds terrible, a manager with a consistently negative IC could theoretically be valuable—you would just do the exact opposite of what they recommend!

In the real world, even very good portfolio managers have surprisingly low ICs, often between 0.05 and 0.10. This sounds tiny, but don't be fooled. A small, consistently positive IC is like having a slight edge in a casino game. Over thousands of hands (or in this case, investment decisions), that small edge compounds into significant, reliable winnings. The IC is the pure, unadulterated measure of a manager's insight. It's their secret sauce, their unique ability to see value where others don't.

Breadth (N): The Opportunity Ingredient 🌐
Now, having a great recipe is one thing, but how many times can you use it? That's where Breadth (N) comes in. Breadth represents the number of independent investment decisions a manager makes over a period.

The key word here is independent.

Imagine a manager who specializes in U.S. auto stocks. They might make a bet on Ford and another on General Motors. Are these two truly independent bets? Not really. Both companies are subject to the same economic cycles, union negotiations, and consumer trends. If the whole auto sector does poorly, both bets will likely fail. This is low breadth.

Now, consider a global macro manager. In a single year, they might make 200 different bets: one on the direction of the Japanese Yen, another on Brazilian interest rates, a third on the price of wheat, a fourth on a German technology stock, and so on. These decisions are largely uncorrelated with each other. A wrong call on wheat prices won't necessarily affect their bet on the Yen. This is high breadth.

The formula uses the square root of N (N), which is a fascinating and crucial detail. It tells us that there are diminishing returns to breadth. This means that going from 1 bet to 10 bets provides a huge boost to your potential. But going from 100 bets to 110 provides a much smaller, incremental benefit. The law encourages making many decisions, but it also acknowledges that each additional decision adds less value than the last. So, a manager's ability to generate alpha isn't just about their skill (IC), but also about how many distinct opportunities they have to apply that skill.

Transfer Coefficient (TC): The Freedom Ingredient

So, you have a skilled manager (good IC) with lots of opportunities (high N). What could possibly go wrong? The answer is: reality. The Transfer Coefficient (TC) measures how effectively a manager can translate their brilliant ideas into an actual portfolio. It's a measure of implementation freedom.

The TC ranges from 1 down to 0.

A TC of 1 represents a perfectly unconstrained manager. Every single idea they have can be put into the portfolio at the exact desired weight. They can short-sell, use leverage, and take concentrated positions without any restrictions. This is the ideal "paper" portfolio.

A TC of 0 means the manager is completely shackled. They might have the best ideas in the world, but rules and restrictions prevent them from acting on any of them.

In practice, almost every manager has a TC of less than 1. Why? Because of constraints. These are the rules of the road that limit a manager's actions. Common constraints include:

No Short Selling: Many traditional funds are "long-only," meaning they can't bet on a stock going down. If a manager's model screams that a company is a terrible investment, the most they can do is not own it (give it a 0% weight). They can't fully express their negative view.

Position Size Limits: A rule might state that no single stock can be more than 5% of the portfolio. What if the manager's best idea is a stock they believe should be 10% of the portfolio? They are constrained.

Benchmark Restrictions: A manager might be required to keep their sector weights within, say, 3% of the benchmark's weights. This prevents them from making big bets on entire sectors they feel strongly about.

Client Mandates: Some clients may impose ESG (Environmental, Social, Governance) restrictions, forbidding investment in tobacco or oil companies, even if the manager's model identifies them as good potential investments.

The TC is the silent killer of active returns. A manager can have world-class skill and a universe of opportunities, but if they are bound by too many rules, their ability to translate that potential into actual performance is severely diminished.

Active Risk (Aggressiveness): Turning Up the Volume 🔊
The Fundamental Law gives us the Information Ratio, which is skill per unit of risk. But how do we get the actual return? We have to multiply that skill by the amount of risk taken. This is often called aggressiveness, or more formally, Active Risk (also known as tracking error).

Expected Active Return = IR × Active Risk

Active risk is the measure of how much a portfolio's returns deviate from its benchmark. A manager who takes on very little active risk is essentially "hugging" the index. Their portfolio will look and perform very much like the benchmark. A manager with high active risk is making big, bold bets. Their portfolio will look very different from the benchmark, and its performance will be much more volatile relative to it.

This final piece shows that the investor has a choice. Once you've found a manager with a good IR (a combination of IC, N, and TC), you can then decide how aggressive you want them to be. If you have high confidence in their skill, you might let them take on more active risk to magnify their potential returns. If you are less certain, you might restrict their active risk to limit the potential for underperformance. It's like having a race car driver with proven skill (high IR); active risk is deciding how hard you want them to press the accelerator.

The Information Ratio as Your Compass: Navigating Manager Selection and Risk

The Fundamental Law isn't just a beautiful theoretical equation; it's an intensely practical tool that serves as a compass for investors. Its primary output, the Information Ratio (IR), is arguably the single most important metric for making two critical decisions: who to hire and how much freedom to give them. It helps you cut through the noise of market performance to find what really matters: skill.

Selecting the Right Manager: Finding True Skill 🏆

In the crowded marketplace of investment managers, everyone can point to a period when they had great returns. But was that success due to genuine skill or just dumb luck? Or perhaps they just took on a ton of risk and happened to be on the right side of the market for a while. The IR helps us distinguish between these scenarios.

Where Active Return is the portfolio's return minus the benchmark's return, and Active Risk (tracking error) is the volatility of that active return. By dividing the return by the risk taken to achieve it, the IR gives us a "risk-adjusted" measure of performance. It tells us how much excess return a manager generates for each unit of risk they take relative to the benchmark. This makes it the ultimate yardstick for comparing managers.

Let's consider a practical example. You are looking to hire a manager to outperform the S&P 500 and have narrowed it down to two candidates:

Manager Alpha: Over the last five years, they have beaten the S&P 500 by an average of 4% per year. However, their active risk was 8%.

Manager Beta: Over the same period, they beat the S&P 500 by a smaller margin, just 3% per year. But they did so with a much lower active risk of 4%.

Who is the more skillful manager? At first glance, Manager Alpha's higher return of 4% might seem more attractive. But the IR tells a different story. Manager Beta is the superior choice. They are far more efficient at converting their insights into performance. For every unit of risk they took, they generated 0.75 units of return, whereas Manager Alpha only generated 0.50. Manager Alpha's higher return was achieved simply by being more aggressive, not by being more skilled. Hiring Manager Beta gives you a more reliable engine of alpha generation.

When using the IR for selection, it's crucial to look for consistency and statistical significance. A high IR over a single year could easily be a fluke. A solid track record should span multiple years and different market environments (bull markets, bear markets, etc.). A good rule of thumb is that an IR of 0.5 is considered good, an IR of 0.75 is very good, and an IR of 1.0 or higher is exceptional and rare over the long term.

Choosing the Right Risk Level: Setting the Aggressiveness Dial 🎛️

Once you've used the IR to identify a skillful manager, the next question is: how much active risk should we let them take? This is a critical decision that directly impacts your potential for outperformance. The IR is the key that unlocks this answer.

The relationship is straightforward:

Expected Active Return = IR × Active Risk

This simple formula allows an investor to set a "risk budget." Let's return to our superior manager, Manager Beta, who we believe has a sustainable IR of 0.75. We can now model our expected outcomes based on different levels of active risk we allow them to take.

Conservative Approach: We might be risk-averse and decide to cap their active risk at 3%.

Expected Active Return = 0.75 × 3% = 2.25%

In this scenario, we are using the manager's skill in a controlled way to aim for a modest but hopefully consistent outperformance.

Moderate Approach: We might be comfortable with a typical level of active risk, say 5%.

Expected Active Return = 0.75 × 5% = 3.75%

Here, we are giving the manager more room to make meaningful bets, targeting a more substantial active return.

Aggressive Approach: If we have very high conviction in the manager's skill and a high tolerance for risk, we could allow an active risk of 7%.

Expected Active Return = 0.75 × 7% = 5.25%

This approach seeks to maximize the reward from the manager's skill, but it comes with the understanding that periods of underperformance could also be more significant.

The IR provides a rational framework for this decision. It separates the manager's skill (the IR, which is relatively stable) from their aggressiveness (the active risk, which is a portfolio construction choice). Without the IR, setting a risk budget is just a shot in the dark. With the IR, it becomes a calculated decision based on the manager's proven ability and the investor's own risk appetite.

In essence, the Information Ratio serves a dual purpose. First, it acts as a quality filter to identify managers who possess genuine, repeatable skill. Second, it acts as a calibration tool, allowing the investor to strategically set the level of risk to align the manager's skill with their own financial goals and comfort level. It transforms the art of active management into a much more transparent and quantifiable science.

Active management is the art and science of trying to beat the market. Unlike passive investing, which simply aims to replicate a market index like the S&P 500, active managers roll up their sleeves and make deliberate bets, believing their skill and insight can lead to superior returns.

This pursuit of "alpha," or excess return, primarily revolves around two core strategies: market timing and security selection. Understanding how these strategies work and how they can be evaluated is crucial for any investor. A powerful, though theoretical, tool for this evaluation is the fundamental law of active management.

Comparing Active Strategies & The Fundamental Law

Imagine you're the captain of a ship sailing across the vast ocean of financial markets. Your goal is to reach your destination (financial goals) faster than all the other ships just drifting with the current (the market index). You have two main ways to gain an edge.

Market Timing: Riding the Waves

Market timing is your macro-level strategy. It's about looking at the sky, checking the barometer, and deciding when to raise your sails to catch a powerful tailwind or when to drop anchor to ride out a storm. In investment terms, this means shifting your money between different asset classes based on broad economic and market forecasts.

A market timer might say, "I believe the economy is heading for a recession, so I'm going to sell most of my stocks and move into the relative safety of government bonds." Six months later, they might declare, "The worst seems to be over, and stocks are cheap. It's time to sell bonds and buy stocks aggressively."

This is a game of big, bold decisions.

Focus: Macroeconomic. It deals with the big picture: interest rates, inflation, GDP growth, and overall market sentiment.

Decisions: Asset Allocation. The key questions are about which asset class to be in—stocks, bonds, commodities, or cash—and when.

Nature of Bets: It involves a small number of very high-impact bets. Getting the direction of the entire stock market right or wrong can make or break your performance for the year.

The allure of market timing is immense; a few correct calls can lead to spectacular returns. However, its difficulty cannot be overstated. Consistently predicting the unpredictable swings of the entire market is exceptionally challenging, and being wrong can be catastrophic.

Security Selection: Finding the Hidden Pearls 💎
If market timing is about predicting the tides, security selection is about sending your divers deep to find specific, undervalued treasures on the ocean floor. This is the classic "stock picking" or "bond picking" strategy. It operates on a micro-level, focusing on the individual merits of a particular company or security.

A security selector isn't as concerned with whether the overall stock market will go up or down tomorrow. Instead, they are obsessed with finding discrepancies between a company's current stock price and its true, underlying (or "intrinsic") value.

They might say, "Regardless of what the broader market does, I believe this specific technology company has a groundbreaking product that the market hasn't fully appreciated yet. Its stock is cheap relative to its future earnings potential, so I'm buying it." At the same time, they might decide to sell shares of another company in the same sector that they believe is overvalued.

Focus: Microeconomic. It involves deep dives into company financial statements, management quality, competitive advantages, and industry trends.

Decisions: Individual Security Choice. The key question is which specific stock or bond to own within an asset class.

Nature of Bets: It typically involves making dozens or even hundreds of smaller, independent bets. The success of the portfolio doesn't hinge on any single stock but on the manager's ability to be right, on average, more often than they are wrong.

Evaluating Strategy with the Fundamental Law of Active Management

So, how can we formally compare these two approaches? Richard Grinold developed a brilliant framework called the fundamental law of active management. It's an elegant equation that breaks down the sources of a manager's success.

Let's break this down into simple terms:

Information Ratio (IR): This is your result. It measures your risk-adjusted active return. A higher IR means you're better at generating returns for the active risk you're taking. It's the ultimate scorecard of an active manager.

Information Coefficient (IC): This is your skill. It measures how well your forecasts correlate with actual outcomes. An IC of 1.0 would mean you have a perfect crystal ball. An IC of 0 means your forecasts are random. A manager who consistently picks stocks that go up has a positive IC.

Breadth (N): This is your opportunity. It represents the number of independent bets you make in a year. "Independent" is the key word—a bet on Coca-Cola and a bet on Pepsi are not truly independent, but a bet on Coca-Cola and a bet on a small biotech firm probably are.

The law provides a powerful lens through which to evaluate a change in strategy.

Let's say a manager decides to shift from market timing to security selection.

The market timer might make only 4 big, independent bets a year (e.g., a quarterly decision on stocks vs. bonds). To be successful, the law tells us they need a very high IC. Let's say their skill (IC) is an impressive 0.20. Their IR would be:

Now, consider a security selector who makes 225 independent stock picks a year. It's much harder to have a high degree of certainty on so many different companies, so their skill (IC) per pick is much lower, say 0.05. Look what happens:

Even though the manager's skill on any single decision is far lower, their overall risk-adjusted performance (IR) is nearly double! They have switched from a strategy reliant on rare, high-conviction insights to one that leverages a small but consistent edge across a vast number of opportunities. This demonstrates why many investment firms favor security selection; it's often more sustainable to have a small edge applied many times than to rely on a few "heroic" calls.

Similarly, if a US-only stock picker decides to expand their strategy to include global stocks, they are directly increasing their Breadth (N). If they can maintain a similar level of skill (IC) in analyzing international companies, the fundamental law predicts their Information Ratio should improve simply because they have more opportunities to apply that skill.

Strengths and Limitations of the Law

The fundamental law is a cornerstone of modern portfolio theory, but it's crucial to understand it as a conceptual framework rather than an infallible scientific formula. It's like a perfectly drawn map of a country—incredibly useful for understanding the terrain, but it doesn't show you where the traffic jams are today.

Practical Strengths: Why It's So Powerful 💪

A Simple, Elegant Framework: The law's greatest strength is its clarity. It brilliantly boils down the messy, complex world of active management into three intuitive components: Skill (IC), Opportunity (Breadth), and Performance (IR). This gives managers a clear vocabulary and a logical structure for thinking about their investment process. It helps answer the fundamental question: "How do we add value?" The answer is to either get better at forecasting (increase IC) or apply our existing skill to more independent opportunities (increase N).

It Champions Diversification of Bets: The most profound practical insight from the law is the mathematical power of breadth. The square root sign in the formula is key; it shows that while you need to quadruple your number of bets to double your IR, the benefit of adding more independent bets is still immense. This has pushed the industry away from overly concentrated portfolios and toward strategies that apply an investment thesis across a wider range of securities, thereby making performance more consistent and less dependent on the outcome of a few big bets.

A Powerful Diagnostic Tool: For a portfolio manager, the law is like a diagnostic check. If a portfolio's performance is lagging (low IR), the manager can use the law to pinpoint the problem. Is our research process flawed and our forecasts are no better than a coin flip (low IC)? Or is our process solid, but we are restricting ourselves to too small a universe of stocks, limiting our ability to deploy our skill (low N)? This helps firms direct resources effectively, whether it's hiring better analysts to improve IC or investing in technology to cover more markets and increase N.

A Better Way to Evaluate Managers: For investors, the law provides a more sophisticated way to assess managers beyond just looking at past returns. An investor can ask a potential manager: "How do you generate your investment insights (your IC)?" and "What is your investment universe and how many independent bets do you typically make (your N)?" A manager who can articulate their process in these terms demonstrates a deeper understanding of how they generate value.

Practical Limitations: Where the Map Diverges from Reality 🗺️

Despite its elegance, the law runs into some significant real-world challenges.

"N" is Nearly Impossible to Measure: This is the law's single biggest weakness. The formula requires the number of independent bets. In the real world, almost nothing is truly independent. Stocks within the same industry move together. Most stocks in a market are influenced by the direction of the overall market (beta). Economic shocks, like a sudden rise in oil prices, affect almost every company. So, is a 500-stock portfolio really 500 independent bets? Absolutely not. The "true N" might be closer to 50 or even less. Estimating this effective number of independent bets is incredibly difficult and a subject of much academic debate, making precise calculation of the formula a practical impossibility.

Skill (IC) is Not a Constant: The law treats the Information Coefficient as a fixed number, but a manager's skill can be frustratingly fickle. A value-investing strategy might produce a great IC during a market recovery but a terrible one during a "dot-com" style speculative bubble. A manager's skill can ebb and flow. The IC is a historical average, but what we really care about is the future IC, which is unknown. This means the law is better at explaining past performance than reliably predicting future performance.

It Ignores Real-World Frictions: The pure version of the law exists in a vacuum free of costs and constraints. In reality, every single bet you add to increase your Breadth comes with transaction costs (brokerage fees, bid-ask spreads). These costs can eat away at the alpha generated. Furthermore, managers face constraints. A manager might be forbidden by their mandate from investing in certain countries or industries. They might want to buy a small-cap stock but find it's too illiquid to build a meaningful position. These frictions can make it impractical or too expensive to fully realize the theoretical benefits of increasing N.

Skill and Breadth Might Not Be Independent: The law assumes you can increase N without affecting IC. Is this always true? Imagine a star analyst who is an expert in U.S. software companies. Their IC for that sector is very high. If their firm tells them to start covering European industrial companies to increase the portfolio's N, it's highly likely their skill (IC) in that new area will be much lower. At some point, expanding breadth can lead to a dilution of skill, a trade-off the basic formula doesn't capture.

In conclusion, the fundamental law of active management is not a magic recipe for beating the market. Its value is not in plugging in numbers and getting a precise answer. Its true and enduring power is as a strategic model. It provides a foundational understanding that a manager's success is a product of their forecasting skill multiplied by the number of times they can effectively apply that skill. It's a compass that points managers in the right direction—toward refining their edge and broadening their horizons—even if it can't draw them a perfect map of the road ahead.

Exchange-Traded Funds: Mechanics and Applications

The creation and redemption process is the behind-the-scenes mechanism that allows Exchange-Traded Funds (ETFs) to trade on an exchange like a stock while maintaining a price close to the actual value of their underlying assets. This entire process is facilitated by special financial institutions called Authorized Participants (APs).

In short, APs create new ETF shares by giving a basket of the underlying securities to the ETF provider in exchange for a large block of ETF shares. They redeem shares by doing the reverse. This continuous creation and redemption by APs acts as an arbitrage mechanism, ensuring the ETF's market price doesn't stray far from its Net Asset Value (NAV), and provides the liquidity we see in the market every day.

The ETF Creation Process: Assembling the Puzzle
Imagine an ETF provider, let's call it "Global Investments," decides to launch a new ETF that tracks the S&P 500 index. They don't just magically make shares appear on the stock market. Instead, they kickstart a sophisticated process that underpins the entire ETF structure, and it all begins with a "recipe." This recipe, officially known as the creation basket, is a precise list of all 500 stocks in the index, down to the exact number of shares of Apple, Microsoft, Amazon, and every other company needed to perfectly mirror the index's composition and weighting. This isn't just a suggestion; it's a strict, non-negotiable blueprint for what constitutes the ETF.

This is where the first key player enters the stage: the Authorized Participant (AP). An AP is not your everyday investor. It's a massive financial institution, typically a large bank or a market-making firm, that has a special legal agreement with Global Investments. Think of the AP as a certified wholesaler with a direct line to the factory. When investor demand for the new S&P 500 ETF starts bubbling up in the market—perhaps the ETF is trading at a slight premium because more people want to buy it than sell it—the AP spots an opportunity.

The AP takes the creation basket (the recipe) from Global Investments and goes on a massive shopping spree in the open market. They purchase every single security on that list, in the exact proportions specified. This is a monumental task, involving acquiring millions of dollars worth of diverse stocks in a very short amount of time. Once the AP has gathered all the necessary ingredients and filled its "shopping cart" with the complete basket of securities, it turns to the ETF provider.

The AP then delivers this entire basket of securities directly to Global Investments. This is an "in-kind" transaction, meaning assets are exchanged for assets, not cash. It's like trading a complete collection of rare comic books for a different, equally valuable collectible. In return for this basket, Global Investments does something unique: it creates a large block of brand-new ETF shares. This block is called a creation unit, which typically consists of 50,000 to 100,000 ETF shares. These shares have just been minted and did not exist moments before. Global Investments hands this creation unit over to the AP.

Now, the AP holds a huge inventory of freshly created ETF shares. What does it do with them? It sells them on the secondary market—the stock exchange where everyday investors like us buy and sell. By introducing this new supply of shares into the market, the AP helps satisfy the high investor demand and, in the process, pushes the ETF's market price back down, closer to its Net Asset Value (NAV), which is the true value of its underlying holdings. The AP pockets a small, risk-free profit from the initial price difference, and the market gains liquidity and efficiency. This creation process happens continuously, day in and day out, ensuring that whenever you want to buy an ETF, there are shares available.

The ETF Redemption Process: Disassembling the Puzzle
Just as there's a carefully orchestrated process for creating ETF shares, there's an equally important one for taking them out of circulation. This is the redemption process, and it's essentially the creation mechanism in reverse. It's the market's self-correcting system for when the supply of an ETF's shares outstrips demand, preventing its price from falling significantly below the actual value of the assets it holds. It ensures the ETF doesn't "break the buck" and trade for less than it's truly worth.

Let's stick with our S&P 500 ETF from Global Investments. Imagine a scenario where a wave of selling hits the market. Perhaps there's some negative economic news, and investors are rushing to sell their holdings. This flood of sell orders could push the ETF's market price down, causing it to trade at a discount to its Net Asset Value (NAV). For example, while the combined value of all the stocks inside the ETF is $100 per share, the ETF itself might be trading on the exchange for just $99.95. For most people, this five-cent difference is negligible, but for an Authorized Participant (AP), this is a flashing green light for a profitable arbitrage opportunity.

The AP, always monitoring for these small price discrepancies, steps into the secondary market. It starts buying up massive quantities of the discounted ETF shares from all the sellers. The AP isn't buying these shares to hold them as a long-term investment; its goal is to accumulate enough of them to form one creation unit—that same large block of 50,000 or 100,000 shares. By buying up all this excess supply on the open market, the AP's actions already begin to put upward pressure on the ETF's price, nudging it back toward its NAV.

Once the AP has amassed a full creation unit, it goes back to the ETF provider, Global Investments. The AP returns this block of ETF shares to the issuer. In exchange, Global Investments doesn't give the AP cash. Instead, it performs another "in-kind" transaction. It hands over the underlying redemption basket of securities—the actual shares of Apple, Microsoft, and all the other 498 companies that were held by the fund. The ETF provider then cancels the ETF shares it received from the AP, and they cease to exist, effectively reducing the total supply of ETF shares available on the market.

The AP is now holding the actual basket of S&P 500 stocks. The final step is for the AP to sell all of these individual stocks on the open market. Since the AP acquired the ETF shares for $99.95 each but received underlying assets worth $100 per share, it locks in a five-cent profit on every single share in that massive creation unit, adding up to a significant, risk-free gain. This redemption process is the market's elegant solution to oversupply. It removes shares from circulation, helps stabilize the price, and ensures that investors can sell their ETF shares at a price that is fair and accurately reflects the value of the assets within the fund.

Authorized Participants: The Arbitrage Guardians of the ETF World 🏛

Authorized Participants, or APs, are the unsung heroes of the Exchange-Traded Fund ecosystem. While investors interact with ETFs on a stock exchange, the APs are the powerful financial institutions working tirelessly behind the curtain, acting as the critical link between the ETF provider (the "factory") and the secondary market (the "storefront"). They are the master mechanics who ensure the entire ETF engine runs smoothly, efficiently, and, most importantly, fairly for all investors. Their primary function is not just to facilitate creations and redemptions but to serve as the guardians of an ETF's price integrity through the power of arbitrage.

At its core, the most vital role of an AP is to keep an ETF's market price in a tight embrace with its Net Asset Value (NAV). The NAV is the per-share value of all the securities held within the ETF, its "true" worth. However, on a stock exchange, the ETF's price is determined by the real-time forces of supply and demand. In a perfect world, these two prices would always be identical, but in reality, they often drift apart by a few pennies throughout the trading day. This tiny difference is called a premium (when the market price is higher than the NAV) or a discount (when the market price is lower). This is where the AP's arbitrage function comes into play.

1. Correcting a Premium: When enthusiastic buying pushes an ETF's price above its NAV, the AP sees a clear arbitrage opportunity. The AP will buy the underlying stocks (the cheaper assets) from the open market, bundle them into a creation basket, and exchange that basket with the ETF provider for newly created, more expensive ETF shares. The AP then immediately sells these new ETF shares on the exchange at the higher market price. The profit is the spread between the two prices. This action increases the supply of ETF shares on the market, which naturally pushes the price back down toward the NAV. The AP makes a profit, and the market becomes more efficient.

2. Correcting a Discount: Conversely, when heavy selling causes an ETF to trade at a discount to its NAV, the AP executes the opposite strategy. It buys the cheap ETF

shares from the stock exchange and redeems them with the ETF provider for the underlying basket of securities, which are inherently more valuable. The AP then sells these individual securities on the market for a profit. This action reduces the number of ETF shares available for trading, decreasing supply and pushing the ETF's market price back up toward its NAV.

Through this constant, profit-driven surveillance, APs act as a powerful stabilizing force. They are the market's self-correcting mechanism, ensuring that the price you pay or receive for an ETF share is an accurate reflection of its intrinsic value. This is a fundamental advantage ETFs have over other fund structures like mutual funds, which are only priced once per day after the market closes. Beyond arbitrage, APs are also essential liquidity providers. Their willingness to create or redeem shares at any time ensures that there is always a deep market for ETFs, allowing investors to easily buy or sell large quantities without significantly impacting the price. They are the ultimate market makers, absorbing supply when investors are selling and providing it when they are buying, which contributes to the tight bid-ask spreads that make ETFs so cost-effective to trade.

ETFs trade on the secondary market just like individual stocks. When you want to buy or sell an ETF, you place an order through a brokerage account. This order is sent to a stock exchange, like the New York Stock Exchange (NYSE), where it's matched with an opposing order from another investor. The price is determined in real-time by supply and demand throughout the trading day. A unique mechanism involving "Authorized Participants" helps keep the ETF's market price very close to the actual value of its underlying assets through a process called creation and redemption.

The Secondary Market Ecosystem: Where the Magic Happens

Imagine your local bustling farmers' market. You have farmers selling their produce (the sellers), shoppers looking for fresh goods (the buyers), and the market square itself (the stock exchange) where all this activity takes place. The secondary market for Exchange-Traded Funds (ETFs) is a lot like this, but instead of apples and oranges, we're trading shares of a fund. This is where the vast majority of ETF trading happens—not with the fund company itself, but between investors like you and me.

The "secondary market" is simply a term for any market where investors buy and sell securities they already own. When a company first offers its stock to the public, that's the primary market. But every trade after that initial offering happens on the secondary market. For ETFs, this is their natural habitat. Once an ETF is launched, its shares are listed on a major stock exchange, such as the NYSE or Nasdaq. This is the central hub, the digital market square where all the action is coordinated.

The key players in this ecosystem are straightforward. First, you have the investors. This includes individual retail investors managing their retirement accounts from their living rooms, as well as massive institutional investors like pension funds and insurance companies managing billions of dollars. We are the shoppers at the market. Then, you have the brokers. Think of them as your personal shopping assistants. When you decide to buy or sell an ETF, you don't call up the stock exchange directly. You place an order through your brokerage account (like Fidelity, Charles Schwab, or Robinhood), and they execute the trade on your behalf. They are the essential link between you and the market.

Finally, at the heart of it all, are the stock exchanges. These are the highly regulated, technologically advanced platforms that facilitate the trading. They operate the complex systems that match buy orders with sell orders in a fraction of a second, ensuring fairness and transparency. They set the rules of the game and provide the infrastructure for this global financial dance to occur smoothly every single trading day. It's a dynamic, interconnected world where millions of transactions happen, all driven by the simple goal of one investor selling a share and another one buying it. This continuous flow of buying and selling is what makes ETFs so accessible and easy to trade for everyone.

The Trading Process: From Click to Confirmation

So, how does a trade actually happen? Let's walk through the journey of a single ETF share as it moves from one investor to another. It's a process that seems instantaneous but involves a fascinating sequence of events happening behind the scenes.

It all starts with a decision. Let's say you've done your research and want to buy 10 shares of an ETF that tracks the S&P 500. You log into your brokerage account, pull up the ETF's ticker symbol (e.g., SPY), and get ready to place an order. You'll immediately see two prices listed: the bid and the ask. The bid price is the highest price a buyer is currently willing to pay for a share, while the ask price is the lowest price a seller is willing to accept. The tiny difference between these two numbers is called the bid-ask spread.

You have a few choices on how to place your order. The simplest is a market order, where you essentially say, "I want to buy 10 shares right now at the best available price." Your broker will immediately fill your order at the current ask price. It's fast and guarantees your trade will execute, but you don't have control over the exact price. Alternatively, you could place a limit order. With a limit order, you specify the maximum price you're willing to pay. For instance, you could say, "I want to buy 10 shares, but only if the price is $450.00 or less." Your order will only be executed if the ETF's price drops to your specified level. This gives you price control but no guarantee that the trade will happen.

Once you hit that "confirm" button, your order is zapped electronically from your broker to the stock exchange. The exchange's powerful matching engine gets to work. It's like a super-fast auctioneer. If you placed a market order, it instantly matches your buy order with the best available sell orders until your 10 shares are acquired. If you placed a limit order, it sits in the order book—a digital ledger of all active buy and sell orders—waiting for a seller to come along who is willing to meet your price.

When a match is found, the transaction is executed. In that split second, ownership of the shares is transferred. You'll see a confirmation pop up in your brokerage account, and the 10 ETF shares are now yours. The cash is debited from your account, and the whole process, from your click to confirmation, is complete, often in less time than it takes to blink. It's a marvel of modern technology that makes investing accessible to millions around the globe.

The Arbitrage Mechanism: Keeping Prices in Check ✅

This is where the real genius behind the ETF structure comes into play, and it's what keeps an ETF's market price from drifting away from the actual value of the assets it holds. The market price of an ETF is determined by supply and demand on the exchange, just like a stock. However, an ETF also has an underlying value, called the Net Asset Value (NAV), which is the total value of all the stocks, bonds, or other assets within the fund's portfolio, divided by the number of shares. In a perfect world, the market price and the NAV would be identical. But in reality, they can briefly diverge. This is where a special group of market players called Authorized Participants (APs) steps in to work their magic through a process called arbitrage.

Think of it like this: Imagine a baker sells a special fruitcake (the ETF). The price of the fruitcake in his shop is set by how many people want to buy it that day. However, the true value of the fruitcake is the combined cost of its ingredients—flour, sugar, fruits, and nuts (the underlying assets or NAV). Now, suppose the fruitcake becomes wildly popular, and people are willing to pay $30 for it in the shop (the market price), even though the ingredients only cost $25 (the NAV).

An AP, which is usually a large financial institution, sees this $5 difference as a risk-free profit opportunity. They won't buy the expensive cake from the shop. Instead, they go to the wholesale market, buy all the ingredients for $25, and use a special deal with the baker to create a brand-new fruitcake. They can then immediately sell this new cake in the shop for the high market price of $30, pocketing a $5 profit. This act of creating a new cake increases the supply in the shop, which naturally pushes the price back down towards the $25 ingredient cost. This is the creation process.

The reverse is also true. If the fruitcake is selling in the shop for just $20 (market price) while the ingredients are still worth $25 (NAV), the AP will do the opposite. They'll buy the cheap cake from the shop for $20, take it to the baker, and exchange it back for the raw ingredients. They can then sell the ingredients on the wholesale market for $25, again making a $5 profit. This is the redemption process. By buying up the cheap cakes, they reduce the supply in the shop, which pushes the price back up towards the $25 ingredient cost.

This continuous creation and redemption mechanism by APs is the invisible hand that ensures an ETF's market price on the exchange stays tightly tethered to its NAV. It's a powerful, self-correcting system that benefits all investors by making sure the price they pay is a fair reflection of the fund's true value.

Liquidity and Spreads: The Unseen Costs of Trading
When you're trading ETFs, two of the most important concepts to understand are liquidity and the bid-ask spread. They are closely related and can have a real impact on your investment returns, even if you don't always notice them directly. Think of liquidity as the ability to buy or sell an asset quickly without causing a major change in its price. An ETF that tracks a popular index like the S&P 500, with millions of shares changing hands every day, is like a deep, wide river—highly liquid. You can easily buy or sell large amounts without disrupting the flow. In contrast, an ETF focused on a very niche, obscure market might be more like a shallow stream—illiquid. A single large trade could cause ripples and significantly move the price.

This level of liquidity directly affects the bid-ask spread we talked about earlier. The spread is essentially the transaction cost you pay to the market makers—the firms that facilitate trading by always being willing to buy (at the bid) and sell (at the ask). For a highly liquid ETF with tons of buyers and sellers, there's a lot of competition, so the spread is usually very tight, often just a penny. The market maker's risk is low because they know they can quickly offload any shares they buy.

However, for an illiquid ETF, the market maker takes on more risk. It might be harder to find a buyer for the shares they acquire, so they have to hold them for longer. To compensate for this risk, they widen the spread. For example, the bid might be $49.90 and the ask $50.10, creating a $0.20 spread. While that doesn't sound like much, it's a cost you pay on every trade. If you buy and then immediately sell, you would lose $0.20 per share just from crossing the spread. Over many trades or with large sums of money, these costs can add up.

So how can you, as an investor, gauge an ETF's liquidity? The most common metric is its average daily trading volume. An ETF that trades millions of shares a day is very liquid. One that trades only a few thousand might be less so. It's also important to remember that an ETF's liquidity isn't just about its own trading volume. It also derives liquidity from its underlying assets. An ETF holding shares of large, actively traded companies will be inherently more liquid than one holding obscure international bonds. By paying attention to volume and understanding the bid-ask spread, you can become a smarter trader, minimizing your transaction costs and ensuring you can get in and out of your positions efficiently and at a fair price.

When you invest in an Exchange-Traded Fund (ETF), you're essentially buying a promise. The promise is that the fund will mirror the performance of a specific market index, like the S&P 500 or the NASDAQ 100, as closely as possible. It's like hiring a professional artist to create a perfect replica of the Mona Lisa. You expect the copy to be virtually indistinguishable from the original. However, just as tiny, almost imperceptible differences in brushstrokes or pigments can separate the replica from the original, small frictions and real-world complexities prevent an ETF from perfectly matching its benchmark index. This performance gap is known as tracking error.

Understanding tracking error is crucial because it measures how well an ETF is doing its fundamental job. While a low tracking error is often the hallmark of a well-managed fund, it's impossible to eliminate it entirely. The sources of this discrepancy aren't mysterious; they are the unavoidable costs and logistical hurdles of turning a theoretical index into a tangible, tradable investment product. Let's delve into the specific factors that create this performance drift.

Fund Expenses and Fees
Perhaps the most straightforward and unavoidable source of tracking error comes from the costs of running the fund itself. Think of an index as a pure, theoretical concept—it's just a list of stocks and their weightings, calculated by a data provider. It has no employees, no office space, and no operating budget. An ETF, on the other hand, is a real-world business with real-world expenses, and these costs directly chip away at the fund's returns, causing it to lag behind its cost-free benchmark.

The most significant of these costs is the management fee, which is captured in the fund's expense ratio. This is the fee you pay the fund manager for their expertise in constructing and maintaining the portfolio, handling legal and compliance duties, and marketing the fund. It's an annual percentage taken directly from the fund's assets. For instance, if an index returns exactly 10% in a year, an ETF tracking it with a 0.10% expense ratio will, all else being equal, return only 9.90%. That 0.10% difference is a direct and predictable form of tracking error.

Beyond the headline management fee, there are other administrative and operational costs. These are the nitty-gritty expenses of keeping the lights on. They include custodian fees (paid to the bank that physically holds the fund's securities for safekeeping), transfer agent fees (for maintaining investor records), legal and accounting fees, and exchange listing fees. While these are typically bundled into the Total Expense Ratio (TER), they represent distinct drags on performance.

Another subtle yet persistent cost is the effect of cash drag. An ETF manager needs to keep a small portion of the fund's assets in cash. This cash buffer is necessary to pay for upcoming expenses and to manage the daily flow of money as investors buy and sell shares of the ETF (a process known as creations and redemptions). The problem is that this cash sits on the sidelines, uninvested. When the stock market is rising, the stocks in the index are appreciating, but the cash held by the ETF is earning next to nothing. This uninvested cash "drags" down the fund's overall performance relative to the fully invested, theoretical index. It's like a sports team trying to win a game with one of its players sitting on the bench—the team simply can't perform at its full potential.

Transaction Costs

Every time an ETF manager needs to buy or sell securities to keep the fund aligned with its index, it incurs transaction costs. The index itself magically rebalances without any friction, but the ETF manager operates in the real world, where every trade has a price tag. These costs, though often small on a per-trade basis, accumulate over time and contribute significantly to tracking error.

This trading is necessary because indexes are not static. Companies are constantly being added or removed, such as when a company gets acquired or no longer meets the criteria for inclusion. Furthermore, the weightings of the existing companies change daily as their market capitalizations fluctuate. To reflect these changes, the ETF manager must rebalance the portfolio by selling stocks whose weights have decreased and buying those whose weights have increased.

The first and most obvious transaction cost is brokerage commissions. Just like an individual investor, the fund has to pay a broker a fee for executing its trades. While large institutions like ETF providers get much better rates than retail investors, the fees are not zero. When an index rebalances quarterly, the ETF might have to execute thousands of trades to mirror the changes, and each one comes with a small commission that eats into returns.

A more subtle but pervasive cost is the bid-ask spread. For any given stock, there are two prices: the "bid" price (the highest price a buyer is willing to pay) and the "ask" price (the lowest price a seller is willing to accept). The ask is always slightly higher than the bid, and the gap between them is the spread. When the ETF buys a stock, it pays the higher ask price. When it sells, it receives the lower bid price. In every round-trip transaction, the fund loses a tiny amount to this spread. Imagine exchanging currency at an airport kiosk; you always buy a foreign currency for a little more and sell it for a little less than the mid-market rate. The index calculation, however, typically uses a single reference price (like the last traded price), completely ignoring this real-world trading friction. For ETFs tracking indexes with many illiquid, less-traded stocks, the bid-ask spreads can be wider and create a more substantial performance drag.

Sampling and Optimization Strategies

The method an ETF uses to replicate its index is a fundamental determinant of its potential tracking error. In a perfect world, every ETF would use full replication. This means the fund would buy every single security in the benchmark index in the exact proportion specified by the index. For an index like the S&P 500, which contains 500 large, liquid U.S. stocks, full replication is the gold standard and is relatively easy to implement. It generally leads to the lowest tracking error because the ETF's portfolio is a near-perfect clone of the index.

However, full replication isn't always practical or even possible. Consider a broad market bond index or an emerging market stock index that contains thousands of individual securities. Some of these components might be very small, illiquid (meaning they don't trade often), or difficult to access. Trying to buy every single one would be incredibly expensive and inefficient. The transaction costs could become so high that they would cause more tracking error than they would prevent.

In these situations, fund managers turn to a strategy called sampling, or optimization. Instead of buying all the securities, the manager purchases a representative sample that is designed to collectively mimic the performance and characteristics (like sector exposure, risk profile, and dividend yield) of the overall index. It's similar to how political pollsters don't need to survey every single citizen to get an accurate picture of national opinion; instead, they carefully select a diverse sample of voters that represents the entire population. The ETF manager will typically buy all the largest and most influential securities in the index and then select a smaller, representative basket of the remaining ones.

The inherent risk of sampling is that the sample's performance might diverge from that of the full index. The manager is making a calculated bet that the securities left out of the portfolio will perform, on average, the same as the ones that were included. But if one of those excluded small-cap stocks suddenly skyrockets due to a takeover bid, the ETF will miss that gain, and its performance will lag behind the index. Conversely, if an omitted stock plummets, the ETF will outperform. This divergence, whether positive or negative, is a direct source of tracking error. The skill of the portfolio manager lies in building a sample that minimizes this risk, but it can never be eliminated entirely.

Other Contributing Factors

Beyond the major drivers of fees, trading costs, and replication strategy, a handful of other, more nuanced factors can create a wedge between an ETF's performance and that of its index. These elements often relate to the handling of dividends, taxes, and unique fund management activities.

A common issue is a mismatch in dividend timing. An index calculation often assumes that dividends are reinvested into the index on the very day a stock goes "ex-dividend." In the real world, the ETF doesn't receive the dividend cash instantaneously. There can be a delay of a day or more between when the dividend is recorded and when the cash actually arrives in the fund's account. During this brief lag, that cash is uninvested and not participating in market movements. If the market rises during this period, the ETF will slightly underperform the index, contributing to tracking error.

Differences in tax treatment, particularly for international ETFs, can be a major source of tracking error. An index's return is typically calculated on a pre-tax basis. However, when an ETF holds foreign stocks, the dividends paid by those companies are often subject to a withholding tax by the foreign government. For example, if a U.S.-based ETF holds a French stock, the French government might withhold a portion of the dividend before it's ever paid to the fund. While tax treaties may allow the fund to reclaim some of this withheld tax, the process can be slow and may not result in a full recovery. This tax drag directly reduces the ETF's return compared to the theoretical, tax-free index.

On the other hand, one activity can actually help reduce tracking error: securities lending. ETF providers can lend out the stocks held in their portfolio to other institutional investors, such as short-sellers, who need to borrow them. In exchange for the loan, the borrower pays a fee to the ETF. This lending revenue acts as extra income for the fund. This income can then be used to help offset the fund's operating costs, such as management fees and transaction costs. A successful securities lending program can be a powerful tool, allowing an ETF to claw back some of the performance lost to expenses. In some cases, the income can be so substantial that it almost completely cancels out the fund's expense ratio, leading to a very small tracking error. This variability in lending revenue, however, introduces another layer of potential difference between the fund and its benchmark.

The bid-ask spread on an Exchange-Traded Fund (ETF) is influenced by four primary factors: the liquidity of the underlying assets held by the ETF, the trading volume of the ETF itself, the costs and risks associated with the creation and redemption process, and overall market volatility. Essentially, the easier and cheaper it is to trade both the ETF and its individual components, the narrower the spread will be.

The Heart of the Matter: Liquidity of Underlying Assets
Imagine an ETF is like a pre-packaged grocery basket. The bid-ask spread of this basket is heavily influenced by how easy it is to buy and sell the individual items inside it. If the basket contains common, everyday items like apples, bread, and milk, a grocer can easily source them and price the basket competitively. This results in a small difference between their buying price (bid) and selling

price (ask). However, if the basket contains rare, exotic fruits from a remote island that are difficult to source, the grocer faces more risk and effort. They will demand a higher selling price to compensate for the trouble, creating a much wider gap.

This is precisely how the liquidity of an ETF's underlying assets works. An ETF that tracks the S&P 500, like the SPDR S&P 500 ETF Trust (SPY), is filled with stocks of massive, publicly traded companies like Apple, Microsoft, and Amazon. These stocks are incredibly liquid—millions of shares are bought and sold every second. For the large financial institutions known as Authorized Participants (APs), whose job is to create and redeem ETF shares, assembling a basket of these stocks is straightforward and cheap. They can buy all 500 stocks with minimal price impact. Because their costs are low and the process is efficient, the resulting bid-ask spread on the ETF itself is razor-thin, often just a single penny.

Now, consider a more specialized ETF, one that invests in corporate bonds from emerging markets or in micro-cap stocks. The assets inside this "basket" are far less liquid. A specific bond from a small company in a developing nation might only trade a few times a week. An AP trying to buy that bond to create a new ETF share might have to pay a premium to entice a seller, or it might take them hours or even days to find one. This difficulty and uncertainty translate directly into higher costs and risks for the AP. To protect themselves, they pass these costs onto investors by widening the bid-ask spread of the ETF. Therefore, when you see a wide spread on an ETF, it's often a direct reflection of the illiquidity of what it holds inside. The spread is essentially the market's way of charging you for the convenience of being able to easily buy and sell a basket of hard-to-trade assets.

Popularity Contest: ETF Trading Volume and Activity

While the contents of the ETF basket are foundational, the popularity of the ETF itself plays an equally crucial role. Think of it as the difference between a bustling city marketplace and a quiet country store. In the crowded city market, you have dozens of vendors selling the same apples. Competition is fierce. If one vendor tries to sell an apple for $2 while everyone else sells it for $1, they won't make any sales. This intense competition forces all vendors to offer very similar prices, narrowing the gap between what buyers are willing to pay and what sellers are asking. This is a market with a tight spread.

An ETF with high trading volume is like that bustling city market. When millions of shares of an ETF trade hands every day, it attracts numerous market makers. These are firms that compete against each other to facilitate trading by constantly posting both a bid price (what they'll pay for the ETF) and an ask price (what they'll sell it for). In a popular ETF, if one market maker posts a spread of $50.00 - $50.05, another will immediately try to win business by offering a better deal, perhaps $50.01 - $50.04. This competitive dynamic is a powerful force that naturally squeezes the spread down to its absolute minimum. The high volume means market makers can trade frequently, earning a tiny profit on each trade but making up for it in sheer quantity. It's a low-risk, high-volume business for them.

Conversely, an ETF with low trading volume is like the quiet country store. There might only be one or two market makers willing to deal in it. With little to no competition, they can set a much wider spread. Why? Because the risk is higher for them. If they buy shares of this unpopular ETF, they might have to hold onto them for a while before another buyer comes along. During that time, the price could drop, causing them to lose money. To compensate for this "inventory risk," they widen the spread. For example, they might offer to buy at $49.90 and sell at $50.10. This 20-cent gap is their buffer, their payment for the risk of dealing in a less popular product. Therefore, a quick look at an ETF's average daily trading volume is a fantastic proxy for its likely bid-ask spread. More traders mean more competition, which means a better deal for you.

Behind the Curtain: The Creation/Redemption Mechanism
The bid-ask spread isn't just a simple matter of supply and demand on the stock exchange; it's deeply connected to the unique plumbing of how ETFs are born and retired. This is the creation and redemption mechanism, and the costs associated with it are a fundamental component of the spread. This process ensures an ETF's market price stays tethered to the actual value of its underlying assets, known as the Net Asset Value (NAV). When this invisible process is costly or inefficient, the spread widens.

Here's how it works: Authorized Participants (APs) are the backstage crew. If demand for an ETF pushes its market price slightly above its NAV, the APs see a profit opportunity. They will step in, buy up all the individual stocks or bonds that the ETF holds directly from the market, bundle them into what's called a "creation unit" (typically a block of 50,000 shares), and exchange this basket with the ETF issuer for brand new ETF shares. They can then sell these new shares on the open market at the slightly higher price for a small, risk-free profit. This act of selling increases the supply of ETF shares, pushing the price back down towards the NAV.

Every step of this process has a cost. The AP has to pay transaction fees (brokerage commissions, exchange fees) to buy hundreds of different securities. For ETFs holding international stocks, there might be currency conversion fees or even foreign taxes. Furthermore, there is hedging risk; in the time it takes the AP to assemble the basket and create the new shares, the prices of those assets could change. The APs factor all of these potential costs—transactional, operational, and hedging—into the price at which they are willing to trade the ETF. These costs form a sort of floor for the bid-ask spread. Even for the most liquid ETF, the spread can't be zero because the APs need to be compensated for their work and risk. For an ETF holding assets in complex, expensive, or highly regulated markets, these creation costs are significantly higher, leading directly to a persistently wider bid-ask spread that investors ultimately pay.

Riding the Waves: Market Volatility and Risk

The final major factor affecting ETF spreads is the temperament of the market itself: volatility. When the market is calm and prices are stable, spreads tend to be tight and orderly. But when fear and uncertainty spike and prices start swinging wildly, bid-ask spreads can blow out dramatically across the board. Volatility is the enemy of certainty, and for market makers, certainty is the name of the game.

Think of a market maker's job as being a professional risk manager. Their goal is to make a small, consistent profit by buying at the bid and selling at the ask. In a stable market, the risk of an asset's price changing drastically in the few seconds they hold it is very low. They can confidently post tight spreads because they know, with a high degree of probability, what the asset will be worth a moment from now.

Now, introduce a sudden geopolitical crisis or a shocking economic news release. The market becomes a chaotic storm. The value of an ETF and all its underlying assets can plummet or soar in the blink of an eye. For a market maker, quoting a price is now incredibly risky. If they offer to buy an ETF at $100.00, its true value could drop to $99.50 before they can offload it, instantly saddling them with a loss. To protect themselves from this immense uncertainty, they do the only logical thing: they widen their spreads. They might back away from the market, quoting a bid of $99.00 and an ask of $101.00. This wide gap acts as a massive financial cushion, giving them a much larger margin of error to absorb any sudden, adverse price movements. This is why you will often see spreads widen significantly during the first few minutes of the trading day (when overnight news is being digested) and during the last few minutes (as positions are being squared away). In essence, the bid-ask spread is a real-time barometer of market risk; the wider it gets, the more uncertainty and fear is coursing through the veins of the financial system.

The Mystery of ETF Premiums and Discounts

Ever looked at an Exchange-Traded Fund (ETF) and seen two different prices? There's the price you see on your screen, changing every second—the market price. Then there's another value, the Net Asset Value (NAV), which is the "official" price of all the stocks or bonds inside the ETF, calculated once a day. Usually, these two prices are almost identical. But sometimes, they drift apart. When the market price is higher than the NAV, the ETF is trading at a premium. When it's lower, it's at a discount.

Think of it like a carefully assembled gift basket. The NAV is the exact cost of all the items inside the basket. The market price is what people are willing to pay for the entire basket right now in a busy marketplace. Sometimes, if that specific basket becomes incredibly popular, people might pay a little extra (a premium) just to get their hands on it immediately. Conversely, if it's less popular, they might only be willing to buy it for slightly less than its contents are worth (a discount).

This gap between the market price and the NAV doesn't just happen by magic. It's caused by a mix of market forces, timing issues, and the nitty-gritty mechanics of how ETFs work.

Sources of the Premium/Discount Puzzle
Several key factors can push an ETF's market price away from its NAV, creating those premiums and discounts.

Timing is Everything: The most common and simplest reason for a small premium or discount is timing. Your brokerage account shows you the ETF's price in real-time, fluctuating with every trade. The NAV, however, is a static snapshot, typically calculated only once after the market closes. During a volatile day, the market might rally or fall significantly in the last few hours. The ETF's price will reflect this movement instantly, but the official NAV is still stuck on yesterday's closing prices for its underlying assets. This lag creates a natural, though usually temporary, gap.

The Human Element: Supply and Demand: Markets are driven by people, and people are driven by emotion. If a particular sector, say, artificial intelligence, suddenly becomes the hottest topic, investors might rush to buy an AI-focused ETF. This surge in demand can push the ETF's market price up faster than its underlying stocks, creating a premium. The opposite is also true. A wave of negative news could cause a sell-off, where a flood of supply from sellers pushes the market price below the NAV, resulting in a discount. This is pure market sentiment at play.

The Liquidity Challenge: An ETF is only as liquid as the assets it holds. The magic that keeps an ETF's price close to its NAV is an arbitrage process done by large institutions called Authorized Participants (APs). If an ETF trades at a premium, APs can buy the underlying stocks, bundle them into new ETF shares, and sell those shares on the market for a profit. This act of creating new shares increases supply and pushes the price back down toward the NAV.

However, what if the ETF holds assets that are hard to buy or sell quickly, like obscure international stocks, real estate, or high-yield "junk" bonds? In this case, it's difficult and costly for APs to perform their arbitrage magic. The process becomes slower and riskier, so they might not step in unless the premium or discount becomes quite large. This inefficiency allows the gap between market price and NAV to widen and persist.

When Markets Sleep: Stale Pricing: This is a big one for international ETFs. Imagine you're in New York trading an ETF that holds Japanese stocks. The New York stock market is open, but the Tokyo stock market has been closed for hours. Let's say positive news about the global economy breaks during the U.S. trading day. Investors will bid up the price of the Japan ETF in anticipation that Japanese stocks will open higher the next day. The ETF's market price will rise. However, its NAV is still being calculated using the old, stale closing prices from Tokyo. This creates a significant premium that reflects the expected future price, not the current locked-in value.

The Taxman Cometh: Occasionally, a potential tax bill can create a discount. ETFs are generally tax-efficient, but they sometimes have to pay out capital gains to shareholders. If a fund is expected to make a large distribution, some investors might sell their shares just before the payout to avoid the tax liability. This selling pressure can temporarily push the ETF's price down, creating a discount.

The Hidden and Not-So-Hidden Costs of Owning an ETF
ETFs are famously celebrated for their low costs compared to traditional mutual funds. While this is largely true, thinking they are "free" is a common mistake. Owning an

ETF involves a handful of distinct costs, some of which are explicit fees, while others are more subtle, embedded in the way you trade and own the fund. Understanding these costs is crucial to managing your investment returns effectively.

Breaking Down the Bill

Let's unpack the different layers of costs you'll encounter when you invest in an ETF.

The Obvious One: The Expense Ratio: This is the most well-known cost. The expense ratio, sometimes called the management fee, is an annual fee that every fund charges to cover its operational expenses. This includes the fund manager's salary, administrative staff, record-keeping, marketing, and other day-to-day costs of running the fund. It's expressed as a percentage of your investment. For example, an expense ratio of 0.10% means you'll pay $1 for every $1,000 you have invested, every year. This fee is automatically deducted from the fund's assets, so you won't see a separate bill; it simply reduces your overall return slightly over time. For broad market index ETFs, these ratios can be incredibly low (under 0.05%), but for more complex or actively managed ETFs, they can be much higher (over 0.75%).

The Trading Toll: The Bid-Ask Spread: This is a cost you pay every single time you buy or sell an ETF. The bid-ask spread is the small difference between the highest price a buyer is willing to pay for a share (the bid) and the lowest price a seller is willing to accept (the ask). For example, if the bid is $100.00 and the ask is $100.02, the spread is two cents. When you place a market order to buy, you'll likely pay the higher ask price. When you sell, you'll receive the lower bid price. This spread is essentially the profit for the market makers who facilitate the trading. For highly popular, high-volume ETFs, this spread can be as narrow as a penny. But for thinly traded, less liquid ETFs, the spread can be much wider, acting as a significant hidden transaction cost.

Brokerage Commissions: The game has changed here, with many online brokers now offering commission-free trading for a wide range of ETFs. However, it's not a universal guarantee. Some brokers might still charge a flat fee, say $4.95, for every trade you make. This can add up quickly, especially if you're investing small amounts or trading frequently. It's crucial to check your broker's fee schedule. Even on "commission-free" platforms, be aware that this usually applies only to online trades; placing an order over the phone with an agent could still incur a fee.

The Premium/Discount Price Tag: As we discussed earlier, buying an ETF at a premium or selling at a discount is a very real cost. If you buy shares when the market price is 1% above the NAV, you have effectively overpaid for the underlying assets by 1%. If you later sell at a 1% discount, you've taken another hit. This cost isn't a fee you pay to the fund company, but rather a cost imposed by market dynamics at the moment of your trade. It highlights the importance of checking the premium/discount status, especially for less liquid ETFs, before placing an order.

Performance Drag: Tracking Error: This isn't a direct fee, but it's a cost in the form of lost performance. Tracking error measures how well an ETF's performance matches the performance of the index it's supposed to track. In a perfect world, if the S&P 500 goes up 10%, your S&P 500 ETF should also go up 10%. In reality, it will likely go up slightly less. Why? The fund's expense ratio is one reason. Another is transaction costs incurred by the fund itself when it has to buy or sell securities to rebalance its portfolio. Some funds use "sampling" strategies, where they only buy a representative sample of the stocks in the index, which can also lead to minor deviations. This small but persistent underperformance is a hidden cost to the investor.

Don't Forget Taxes: ETFs are known for being highly tax-efficient, primarily because their creation/redemption mechanism allows them to avoid realizing capital gains when investors sell shares. However, they are not tax-free. When you sell your ETF shares for a profit, you will owe capital gains tax on that profit, just like with an individual stock. Additionally, the dividends paid out by the stocks within the ETF are passed on to you and are typically taxed as ordinary income or as qualified dividends.

Navigating the Waters: Understanding the Risks of ETFs
Exchange-Traded Funds (ETFs) have exploded in popularity, and for good reason. They offer a simple, low-cost way to invest in a whole basket of assets, like stocks or bonds, with a single purchase. Think of it like buying a pre-packaged grocery bag filled with all the ingredients for a week's meals instead of having to pick out every single item yourself. It's convenient and efficient. However, just like any journey into the financial markets, investing in ETFs isn't without its potential storms and hidden currents. Understanding these risks is the first step to becoming a savvy and confident investor.

The Big One: Market Risk
This is the granddaddy of all investment risks and the one that affects nearly every ETF. Market risk, also known as systemic risk, is the possibility that the entire market or a large segment of it will decline, taking your ETF's value down with it. It's like being in a boat on the ocean; when the tide goes out, all the boats go down, regardless of how well-built they are.

This risk has nothing to do with the specific companies in the ETF. Instead, it's driven by broader economic shifts, geopolitical events, changes in interest rates, or even just widespread investor panic. For example, if you own an ETF that tracks the S&P 500, a major stock market index in the US, and the entire US stock market tumbles due to recession fears, the value of your ETF will fall accordingly. You can't diversify this risk away completely because it's inherent to being in the market. The only way to avoid it is to not invest at all, which comes with its own risk of losing purchasing power to inflation.

The Annoying Sibling: Tracking Error Risk
One of the main selling points of an ETF is that it's designed to mirror the performance of a specific index, like the NASDAQ 100 or a global bond index. However, in the real world, achieving a perfect mirror image is nearly impossible. The small difference between an ETF's performance and its index's performance is called tracking error.

So, what causes this gap? A few things. First, fees and expenses. The ETF has management fees and operational costs that the index doesn't, which slightly drag down the ETF's return over time. Second, there's something called cash drag. ETFs often hold a small amount of cash to handle investor redemptions or to wait for the right moment to invest new money. This cash isn't invested in the index's assets, so if the market is soaring, that uninvested cash isn't earning the same returns, creating a slight performance lag. Finally, some ETFs, especially those tracking massive indexes with thousands of stocks, use a technique called "sampling." Instead of buying every single security in the index, the fund manager buys a representative sample that they believe will perform just like the full index. Most of the time it works well, but sometimes the sample doesn't behave exactly like the whole, leading to tracking error.

The Rush Hour Traffic Jam: Liquidity Risk

Liquidity refers to how easily you can buy or sell something without dramatically affecting its price. With ETFs, liquidity risk is a two-lane highway.

On one side, you have the liquidity of the ETF shares themselves. For popular, high-volume ETFs that track major indexes, this is rarely a problem. There are always tons of buyers and sellers, so you can trade your shares in a flash. But for more niche, thinly-traded ETFs (like one that focuses on a very specific sub-sector of the Turkish economy), there might not be many people looking to trade at any given moment. In this case, you might have to sell for a lower price than you'd like (a wide bid-ask spread) or wait longer to find a buyer.

On the other side of the highway is the liquidity of the underlying assets the ETF holds. This is a sneakier risk. An ETF might trade frequently, but if it holds assets that are themselves hard to sell—like certain high-yield "junk" bonds or real estate in a slow market—it can run into trouble. During a market panic, if many investors try to sell the ETF at once, the fund manager has to sell those illiquid underlying assets to raise cash. If they can't sell them quickly or have to sell them at fire-sale prices, it can cause the ETF's market price to plummet far below the actual value of its holdings.

The Trust Factor: Counterparty & Structural Risks

Imagine you made a deal with a friend, but then your friend can't hold up their end of the bargain. That's essentially counterparty risk. This risk is most prominent in "synthetic" ETFs. Unlike traditional ETFs that physically own the assets in their index, synthetic ETFs use derivatives, like a swap agreement with a big investment bank. The bank promises to deliver the return of the index to the ETF. The risk? If that bank goes bust, the ETF could be left with a worthless contract, and investors could lose their money. While rare, it's a critical risk to be aware of, especially with more complex products.

Structural risks relate to how the ETF is built and trades. ETFs have two prices: the market price (what you pay on the stock exchange) and the Net Asset Value or NAV (the real-time value of all its underlying assets). A clever mechanism involving "authorized participants" usually keeps these two prices very close. However, during moments of extreme market volatility, the mechanism can break down. This can lead to the ETF's market price trading at a significant premium (higher than its NAV) or discount (lower than its NAV), meaning you could pay more than it's worth or sell for less.

The Swiss Army Knife of Investing: Portfolio Uses of ETFs

Just as a Swiss Army knife has a tool for almost any situation, ETFs have become the ultimate multipurpose tool for modern investors. Their flexibility, low cost, and transparency allow them to be used in a huge variety of ways to build, adjust, and protect a portfolio. Whether you're a hands-off beginner or a seasoned market strategist, there's a way to put ETFs to work for you. 🛠️

The Foundation: Core Holdings and Diversification

The most fundamental use of ETFs is to build the very foundation of an investment portfolio. This is often called a "core" holding. The goal here is simple: achieve broad diversification instantly and cheaply. Instead of painstakingly researching and buying hundreds of individual stocks, you can buy a single broad-market ETF.

For example, an ETF that tracks the MSCI World Index gives you a slice of thousands of companies across dozens of developed countries. One transaction, and you're diversified globally. This approach forms the stable, long-term center of your portfolio. It's like building a house; you need a solid, wide concrete foundation before you start putting up the walls and decorating the rooms. These core ETFs are designed to capture the general return of the market over the long run, providing the bedrock upon which all other investment decisions are made. This is the classic "buy and hold" strategy, simplified for the modern age.

The Architect's Blueprint: Asset Allocation & Core-Satellite Strategy

Once your foundation is laid, ETFs are the perfect building blocks for constructing your desired asset allocation. Asset allocation is simply the art of deciding how to split your money among different types of investments, or asset classes—primarily stocks, bonds, and alternatives like commodities or real estate. This decision is the single biggest driver of your portfolio's long-term returns and risk level.

ETFs make this process incredibly easy. Want 60% in stocks and 40% in bonds? You can buy a global stock ETF and a global bond ETF in those proportions. Need to add a 5% allocation to gold to hedge against inflation? There's an ETF for that. Need to increase your exposure to emerging markets? There's an ETF for that, too.

This leads to a popular and powerful portfolio design called the "core-satellite" strategy. Your "core" (as described above) is your large, diversified holding that you rarely touch. Your "satellites" are smaller, more targeted ETF positions that you use to express specific views or chase higher returns. For instance, if you believe the healthcare sector is poised for growth due to an aging population, you could add a healthcare sector ETF as a satellite. If you think Japanese stocks are undervalued, you could add a Japan-focused ETF. This strategy gives you the best of both worlds: a stable, diversified base combined with the flexibility to make tactical bets without disrupting your entire portfolio.

The Tactical Playbook: Sector Rotation, Thematic Investing, and Hedging

For more active investors, ETFs are invaluable tactical tools. Their liquidity—the ability to be bought and sold throughout the trading day like a stock—makes them perfect for making quick adjustments to a portfolio.

This is especially useful for sector rotation. The economy moves in cycles, and different sectors perform better at different stages. During an economic expansion, cyclical sectors like technology and consumer discretionary might do well. During a downturn, defensive sectors like utilities and consumer staples tend to hold up better. An active manager can use sector-specific ETFs to overweight the sectors they believe are about to outperform and underweight those they think will lag, all without having to buy dozens of individual stocks.

ETFs are also the primary vehicle for thematic investing. This involves investing in long-term trends that are reshaping the world, like artificial intelligence, clean energy, robotics, or cybersecurity. ETFs bundle together companies that are poised to benefit from these powerful themes, giving investors a simple way to invest in the future.

Finally, ETFs can be used for hedging and risk management. Let's say you have a large portfolio of tech stocks and you're worried about a short-term correction. You could buy an "inverse ETF" that is designed to go up when the tech sector goes down, effectively providing some insurance for your portfolio. Or, if you're holding a lot of cash waiting for an opportunity but don't want to miss out on potential market gains, you can temporarily "park" that money in a highly liquid broad-market ETF. This process, known as "equitizing cash," keeps you invested while you make your next move. From foundational building to precision tactical maneuvers, ETFs truly offer a tool for every investor's needs.

Using Multifactor Models

Arbitrage Pricing Theory (APT): A Different Way to Look at Risk and Return
Imagine you're trying to figure out the "fair" price or expected return on a stock. One famous tool for this is the Capital Asset Pricing Model (CAPM). It's elegant but a bit of a one-trick pony; it suggests that the only risk that matters is the overall market risk, often called beta. But is that really how the world works? 🤔 What about things like surprise inflation announcements, sudden shifts in interest rates, or a spike in oil prices? Don't these things also rock the financial boat and affect stock prices?

This is where Arbitrage Pricing Theory (APT), developed by economist Stephen Ross in 1976, enters the scene. APT is a more flexible and, some would argue, a more realistic model for explaining asset returns. Instead of pinning everything on a single factor (the market), APT proposes that an asset's return is influenced by multiple systematic risk factors.

Think of it like baking a cake. 🎂 CAPM says the taste of the cake (the stock's return) depends only on the amount of flour (market risk) you use. APT, on the other hand, says the taste is a result of a combination of ingredients: flour, sugar (inflation risk), eggs (interest rate risk), and vanilla extract (industrial production changes). Each ingredient has a different impact, and APT tries to measure the sensitivity of the cake's flavor to each one.

The core idea of APT is that the expected return of a financial asset can be modeled as a linear function of various macroeconomic factors, where sensitivity to changes in each factor is represented by a factor-specific beta coefficient. The model doesn't specify what these factors must be, which is both a strength (flexibility!) and a weakness (ambiguity!). Researchers have to use statistical analysis to identify the factors that seem to be driving returns in the market. Common candidates often include:

Unexpected inflation: How much do rising prices eat into your investment's value?

Changes in industrial production: A booming economy is generally good for stocks.

Shifts in the yield curve: Changes in the difference between short-term and long-term interest rates can signal economic shifts.

Changes in investor confidence: Sometimes, the overall mood of the market matters.

Underlying Assumptions of APT

Every financial theory rests on a foundation of assumptions, and APT is no different. These assumptions are crucial because they create the perfect world in which the theory holds true.

Systematic Factors Drive Returns: The most fundamental assumption is that asset returns are explained by a linear relationship with a set of common macroeconomic (systematic) factors. The model also includes an error term to capture firm-specific (unsystematic) risk, like a factory fire or a major lawsuit.

Diversification Eliminates Unsystematic Risk: APT assumes that investors hold well-diversified portfolios. In a large, diversified portfolio, the random, firm-specific good news and bad news from different companies cancel each other out. This means that unsystematic risk effectively disappears, and the only risk that matters is the systematic risk that affects the whole market. You can't diversify away a recession!

No Arbitrage Opportunities Exist: This is the big one. The theory is built on the idea that financial markets are efficient enough to eliminate "free lunches." An arbitrage opportunity is a situation where you can make a risk-free profit with zero initial investment. The model assumes that if such an opportunity were to arise, smart investors would jump on it instantly. Their trading activity would cause prices to adjust until the opportunity vanished. This "no-arbitrage" condition is what forces assets with the same risk exposures to have the same expected return.

Relation to Multifactor Models

So how does APT relate to multifactor models? Think of it this way: APT is the theoretical justification, while a multifactor model is the practical application.

APT provides the powerful, elegant theory that says an asset's return should be based on its exposure to multiple systematic risks. It gives us the "why." However, it doesn't name the specific factors.

A multifactor model takes this theoretical framework and runs with it. It's an attempt to build a concrete, usable version of APT by identifying specific factors that explain returns. The most famous example is the Fama-French Three-Factor Model, which proposes that stock returns are explained by:

Overall market risk (just like CAPM).

The "size" factor (small-cap stocks tend to outperform large-cap stocks).

The "value" factor (high book-to-market ratio "value" stocks tend to outperform "growth" stocks).

So, while APT is the general theory (returns are driven by multiple factors), the Fama-French model is a specific hypothesis about what some of those factors are. Any model that uses multiple variables to explain asset returns is a multifactor model, and it stands on the theoretical shoulders of the Arbitrage Pricing Theory. In essence, APT is the parent theory, and multifactor models are its operational children.

The Elusive "Free Lunch": Arbitrage Opportunities

In the world of finance, an arbitrage opportunity is the ultimate prize—it's the equivalent of finding a winning lottery ticket on the ground. 💰 It represents a chance to make a guaranteed, risk-free profit with absolutely no money down. Sounds too good to be true, right? Well, in efficient markets, it usually is. But understanding what it is and how to spot it is fundamental to modern finance.

At its core, arbitrage is the act of exploiting a price difference between two or more markets for the same asset. The principle that prevents this is called the Law of One Price, which states that identical assets should have the same price everywhere. If a stock is trading for $10 on the New York Stock Exchange and $10.05 on the London Stock Exchange (after accounting for exchange rates), an arbitrageur could simultaneously buy it in New York and sell it in London, pocketing the 5-cent difference per share.

Formally, an arbitrage opportunity is a trading strategy that satisfies one of the following three conditions:

You make a positive, risk-free profit today with zero net investment.

You receive money today with zero risk of having to pay anything back in the future.

You invest nothing today, face no possibility of a future loss, and have a positive chance of a future gain.

The simplest definition to remember is this: a zero-investment portfolio that generates a positive, risk-free return. The "zero-investment" part is key. You achieve this by balancing a long position (buying an undervalued asset) with a short position (selling an overvalued asset). The cash you get from the short sale funds your purchase of the long position, so you don't have to put up any of your own capital.

Imagine two portfolios, Portfolio A and Portfolio B. They have the exact same exposure to all systematic risk factors (e.g., inflation, interest rates). According to the no-arbitrage principle of APT, they must have the same expected return. If Portfolio A has an expected return of 12% and Portfolio B has an expected return of 14%, an arbitrage opportunity exists. Why? Because you've found two identical items with different price tags.

How to Determine if an Arbitrage Opportunity Exists
So, how do you mathematically hunt for one of these opportunities? It involves a bit of detective work and some straightforward algebra. Let's walk through an example.

Suppose we are in a world where stock returns are explained by just two factors: surprises in GDP growth (Factor 1) and unexpected changes in inflation (Factor 2). The risk-free rate is 3%.

Export to Sheets
The question is: Is there a mispricing here? Does an arbitrage opportunity exist?

Step 1: Find the Factor Risk Premiums

First, we need to figure out what the market is paying investors for taking on the risk of each factor. We can use the APT equation and the information from two of the portfolios to solve for the risk premiums

Step 2: Check for Mispricing

Now we use this pricing equation to calculate the "fair" or theoretical expected return for Portfolio Z. If the theoretical return doesn't match its actual expected return, we've found our arbitrage opportunity.

Wait a minute. The theoretical return for Portfolio Z is 10%, and its actual expected return is also 10%. In this case, no arbitrage opportunity exists. Portfolio Z is priced correctly according to the risk premiums set by Portfolios X and Y.

Step 3 (Hypothetical): What if there WAS a mispricing?

Let's change the scenario slightly. What if Portfolio Z's actual expected return was 12% instead of 10%?

Actual Return = 12%

Theoretical (Fair) Return = 10%

Here, Portfolio Z is undervalued. It's offering a higher return than its risk profile warrants. An arbitrage opportunity exists! Here's how you'd exploit it:

Construct a Replicating Portfolio: Create a new portfolio (let's call it "RP") using Portfolios X and Y that has the exact same risk profile (betas) as Portfolio Z. We need to find weights

Execute the Arbitrage:

Short Sell the overpriced asset (or, in this case, the combination of assets that gives the fair price). You would short sell the Replicating Portfolio (RP).

Buy the undervalued asset. You would buy Portfolio Z.

By shorting $100 of RP and buying $100 of Z, you have a zero-investment portfolio. Your risk exposures are perfectly hedged because the betas of the long and short positions cancel out. But what about the profit?

Profit = Return on Long Position - Return on Short Position
Profit = $12 (from Z) - $10 (from RP) = $2.

You have just made a guaranteed, risk-free profit of $2 on a zero-dollar investment. That, right there, is the magic of arbitrage. In the real world, this activity would quickly drive up the price of Z (lowering its future expected return) and drive down the prices of X and Y (raising their future expected returns) until the 12% anomaly disappeared and all three portfolios lined up on the same pricing plane.

Calculating an Asset's Expected Return

Imagine you're trying to figure out the potential reward for making an investment. You wouldn't just guess, would you? You'd want to understand what drives that investment's performance. That's precisely what a multifactor model helps us do. It's like a recipe for an asset's return, telling us which "ingredients"—or factors—contribute to the final result and in what quantities. Calculating the expected return is essentially following this recipe to see what the outcome should be.

At its core, the calculation is a beautiful and intuitive piece of financial logic. It starts with a baseline and then adds on extra returns for each specific risk the asset is exposed to.

The Building Blocks of Expected Return

The Risk-Free Rate (R_f): This is our foundation. It's the return you could earn on a theoretically "zero-risk" investment, like a U.S. Treasury bill. Why do we start here? Because any investment should, at the very least, compensate you for the time your money is tied up. This is the bare minimum return you'd demand even if there were no risk involved at all. It's the price of just waiting.

The Factor Risk Premium (RP_j): These are the rewards for taking on specific, unavoidable risks. The market doesn't reward every risk, only the ones you can't diversify away (these are called systematic risks). A factor risk premium is the extra return, on average, that investors demand for bearing the uncertainty associated with a particular economic or market force. For instance, there's a risk that the whole economy could slow down (GDP risk), or that inflation could spike unexpectedly. For each of these persistent, market-wide risks, investors require a "premium" or a little extra return as compensation for putting up with that uncertainty.

The Factor Sensitivity (β_{ij}): This is the most crucial, dynamic part of the recipe. The beta tells us how much a specific asset (i) is affected by a specific factor (j). It's a measure of reactivity or sensitivity. A beta of 1 means the asset moves in perfect sync with the factor. A beta of 2 means it's twice as sensitive—if the factor's premium is positive, the asset gets double the benefit, but if it's negative, it takes double the hit. A beta of 0 means the factor has no impact on the asset. And a negative beta means the asset moves in the opposite direction of the factor, which can be a great thing for diversifying a portfolio!

Let's Cook Up an Expected Return: A Step-by-Step Example

Let's make this tangible. Imagine we're analyzing a hot tech stock called "FutureGadget Inc." We want to calculate its expected annual return using a three-factor model.

Step 1: Identify the Baseline and the Risk Factors

Our model uses three systematic risk factors that we believe drive the market:

Factor 1: Economic Growth Surprise. This factor captures unexpected changes in GDP. The market rewards stocks that do well when the economy booms. The Risk Premium for Economic Growth (RP GDP) is 5%.

Factor 2: Interest Rate Surprise. This captures unexpected moves in interest rates by the central bank. Rising rates can hurt some stocks. The Risk Premium for Interest Rates (RP INT) is -1% (meaning, on average, exposure to this risk has been a drag on returns).

Factor 3: Market Momentum. This captures the tendency of winning stocks to keep winning. The Risk Premium for Momentum (RP
MOM) is 3%.

Step 2: Determine FutureGadget's Sensitivities (Betas)

Now, we need to know how sensitive FutureGadget is to each of these factors. After some statistical analysis, we find:

Beta to Economic Growth (β GDP) is 1.4. This makes sense. As a growing tech company, its sales are highly dependent on a strong economy, so it's more sensitive than the average company (which would have a beta of 1).

Beta to Interest Rates (β INT) is -0.8. This means FutureGadget tends to do well when interest rates unexpectedly fall. This is common for growth stocks, as lower rates make their distant future profits more valuable today.

Beta to Market Momentum (β MOM) is 0.7. It has positive momentum but is slightly less sensitive to this factor than the average high-momentum stock.

Step 3: Put It All Together in the Formula

Let's substitute the numbers:

$E(R \text{ FutureGadget }) = 2\% + (1.4 \times 5\%) + (-0.8 \times -1\%) + (0.7 \times 3\%)$

Step 4: Calculate the Result

Now, we just do the math, one piece at a time:

Contribution from Economic Growth: $1.4 \times 5\% = 7.0\%$

Contribution from Interest Rates: $-0.8 \times -1\% = +0.8\%$ (The double negative makes it positive!)

Contribution from Momentum: $0.7 \times 3\% = 2.1\%$

Finally, add everything to the risk-free rate:

$E(R \text{ FutureGadget }) = 2\% + 7.0\% + 0.8\% + 2.1\% = 11.9\%$

Our calculated expected return for FutureGadget Inc. is 11.9%. This number tells us what we can anticipate earning from this stock over the next year, given its specific risk exposures and the market's compensation for those risks. It's a powerful tool that moves beyond a simple guess and gives us a reasoned, analytical expectation.

A Tale of Three Models: Macroeconomic, Fundamental, and Statistical

In the quest to explain what makes stock prices move, financial minds have developed three distinct families of factor models. While they all share the same goal—to explain investment returns using underlying factors—their philosophies and methods are worlds apart. Think of them as three different detectives trying to solve the same mystery, each with a unique approach to gathering and interpreting clues.

The Macroeconomic Factor Model: The Economist Detective 🕵️

This model is the "top-down" investigator. It starts with the big picture, believing that the most important drivers of asset prices are broad economic forces that ripple through the entire system. This detective looks at surprise announcements you'd hear about in the financial news.

Description: Macroeconomic models assert that an asset's return is sensitive to unexpected changes (or "shocks") in major economic variables. The key word here is unexpected. The market has already priced in what it expects to happen (e.g., everyone expects 2% inflation). It's the surprise (e.g., inflation suddenly jumps to 4%) that causes stock prices to adjust.

The Factors: The factors are observable, real-world economic data points. Common examples include:

Changes in the Gross Domestic Product (GDP)

Unexpected inflation

Shifts in the yield curve (the difference between long-term and short-term interest rates)

Changes in unemployment rates

Consumer confidence levels

How It Works: The analyst first chooses which economic variables they believe are the most influential. Then, using historical data, they run a time-series regression to estimate the sensitivity (beta) of a specific asset to surprises in each of these variables.

Analogy: Imagine being a ship's captain. A macroeconomic model is like understanding that your ship's speed is affected by the major ocean currents (GDP), the wind (inflation), and the height of the tides (interest rates). You are trying to figure out how much your specific ship is pushed around by a sudden, unexpected gust of wind or a change in the current.

Strength: It's highly intuitive. The factors make clear economic sense, making it easy to tell a story about why a portfolio performed a certain way.

Weakness: It requires identifying all the right macroeconomic factors, and sometimes the market is influenced by things that aren't easily captured by these big, slow-moving variables.

The Fundamental Factor Model: The Stock Analyst Detective 🕵

This model is the "bottom-up" investigator. It couldn't care less about the broad economy, at least not directly. Instead, this detective goes straight to the source, examining the specific characteristics—the fundamentals—of the companies themselves.

Description: Fundamental models argue that returns are driven by attributes related to a company's financial health, valuation, and market perception. These are not abstract economic forces but tangible company data.

The Factors: The factors are company-specific attributes. Famous examples come from the Fama-French models, which include:

Size: The company's market capitalization (e.g., Small-Cap vs. Large-Cap).

Value: How cheap the stock is relative to its fundamentals (e.g., a low Price-to-Book ratio).

Growth: Indicators of a company's growth potential.

Quality: Measures of financial health, like profitability or low debt.

Momentum: The stock's recent price performance.

How It Works: In this case, the betas (sensitivities) are not estimated from a regression. They are simply the values of the attributes themselves, often standardized. For example, a company with a very low price-to-book ratio would have a high sensitivity to the "Value" factor. The model then looks at a cross-section of all stocks at a point in time to calculate the risk premium, or the return earned, for each of these fundamental attributes.

Analogy: Think of it like building a basketball team. A fundamental model doesn't care about the league's overall TV ratings (the macroeconomy). It explains your team's success by looking at the attributes of your players: how tall they are (Size), how underrated they are (Value), and how many games they've won recently (Momentum).

Strength: It is incredibly useful for portfolio construction and style analysis, helping managers understand if their portfolio is tilted towards, say, "small-cap value" or "large-cap growth."

Weakness: The factors themselves might just be proxies for underlying, unnamed macroeconomic risks. The economic rationale for why, for example, "value" stocks should outperform over the long run is still debated.

The Statistical Factor Model: The Data Scientist Detective 🤖

This model is the most agnostic and data-obsessed of the three. It walks into the crime scene with no preconceived theories. It doesn't look at economic reports or financial statements. It just looks at one thing: the raw historical return data of all the assets.

Description: Statistical models let the data do all the talking. They use statistical techniques, like Principal Component Analysis (PCA), to sift through a massive matrix of asset return data and identify the underlying patterns or "factors" that best explain why stocks tend to move together.

The Factors: The factors are not chosen; they are extracted by the statistical process. The model might spit out "Factor 1," "Factor 2," and "Factor 3." These are abstract, mathematical portfolios that explain the maximum amount of variance in the data.

How It Works: The computer analyzes the historical co-movement of hundreds or thousands of stocks. It finds the most dominant, independent patterns of movement. For example, it might find that one pattern ("Factor 1") explains 30% of all stock movements, another ("Factor 2") explains 10%, and so on.

Analogy: Imagine monitoring thousands of cell phones in a city. A statistical model doesn't know why people are moving, but it can identify common patterns. It might detect a "morning commute factor" where thousands of phones move from residential areas to the downtown core, and an "evening entertainment factor" where they cluster in restaurant districts, all without needing to know a single person's individual plans.

Strength: It can uncover complex, hidden risk factors that the other models, with their human-specified factors, might miss. It is free from the bias of choosing the "wrong" factors.

Weakness: The massive, glaring weakness is interpretation. The model might tell you that your portfolio has a high sensitivity to "Factor 1," but you have no idea what Factor 1 actually is. Is it some combination of inflation and value? Is it related to global trade? It's often a "black box," which makes it difficult for humans to understand, trust, and build an economic narrative around.

In the end, no single model is universally superior. They are different lenses through which to view the complex world of financial markets. An economist might favor the macroeconomic model, a portfolio manager the fundamental model, and a quantitative analyst the statistical model. Each provides a unique and valuable perspective on the enduring mystery of what drives returns.

Unpacking Multifactor Models: What They Are and How to Read Them

Imagine trying to predict the weather by only looking at the temperature. You'd get part of the picture, right? But you'd miss crucial details like humidity, wind speed, and atmospheric pressure. In the same way, trying to understand a stock's return by only looking at one factor, like the overall market movement, is incomplete. This is where multifactor models come into play. They are the financial world's version of a complete weather report, giving us a much richer, more nuanced understanding of why asset prices move the way they do.

What Are Multifactor Models Used For?

At their core, multifactor models are tools that help us explain and predict investment returns. Instead of saying a stock went up just because "the market went up," these models say, "Well, yes, the market helped, but the stock also performed well because it's a 'value' stock in a period when value is favored, and it's a smaller company, which also saw positive momentum." It's all about breaking down performance into its fundamental drivers.

Here are their main uses:

Return Attribution: This is a big one. After a portfolio manager has had a successful year, the client naturally asks, "How did you do it?" A multifactor model can dissect the returns and pinpoint the sources of success. Was it skill in picking specific stocks? Or was the manager simply riding a wave by being invested in, say, high-growth tech stocks when that sector was booming? This process separates genuine skill (alpha) from just being exposed to the right market forces (beta).

Risk Management: Understanding your risks is paramount. A multifactor model acts like an X-ray for your portfolio. It can reveal hidden concentrations of risk you might not be aware of. For instance, you might think you have a diversified portfolio of 50 different stocks. But a multifactor analysis could show that 40 of them are highly sensitive to changes in interest rates or oil prices. Suddenly, your "diversified" portfolio doesn't seem so diverse after all. It helps you see the types of economic weather your portfolio is exposed to.

Portfolio Construction: Armed with this deeper understanding of risk and return drivers, managers can build more robust and targeted portfolios. Want to create a portfolio that specifically benefits from economic growth? You can screen for stocks with high sensitivity to a GDP growth factor. Trying to build a defensive portfolio? You might look for stocks with low sensitivity to market volatility. It's like being a chef who can precisely choose ingredients (factors) to create a specific flavor profile (portfolio).

Interpreting the Output: Making Sense of the Numbers

When you run a multifactor model analysis, you typically get an output that looks something like this for a specific asset or portfolio:

Let's break this down into simple English:

(The Excess Return): This is simply the return of your portfolio (R_p) over and above the risk-free rate (R_f), like what you'd get from a government bond. It's the return you got for taking on risk.

The Factors (F 1 ,F 2 ,...): These are the "ingredients" or economic forces we believe drive returns. Common examples include:

Market Factor (MKT): The overall stock market's excess return.

Size Factor (SMB - "Small Minus Big"): The return of small-cap stocks minus the return of large-cap stocks.

Value Factor (HML - "High Minus Low"): The return of value stocks (high book-to-market ratio) minus the return of growth stocks (low book-to-market ratio).

Momentum Factor (MOM): The return of stocks that have performed well recently minus those that have performed poorly.

A beta of 1.2 for the market factor means that if the market goes up by 10%, you'd expect your portfolio to go up by 12%, all else being equal.

A positive beta for the value factor (HML) means your portfolio is tilted towards value stocks. It will tend to do well when value stocks outperform growth stocks.

A negative beta for the size factor (SMB) suggests your portfolio is dominated by large-cap stocks.

Alpha (α): This is the magic number. It represents the portion of the portfolio's return that cannot be explained by any of the factors in the model. It's often considered the measure of a manager's true skill—their ability to generate returns beyond just riding market trends. A positive and statistically significant alpha is the holy grail for active managers.

Epsilon (ϵ): This is the error term, representing the random, unpredictable noise or the portion of the return that is specific to the individual stocks and not captured by the broad factors.

So, when you look at the output, you're essentially reading a story about your portfolio. You're seeing how much of its performance came from the general market tide, how much came from its tilt towards small companies or value companies, and most importantly, how much—if any—came from the unique insights of the person managing it.

Beyond a Single Lens: The Power of a Multi-Dimensional Risk View

For decades, the investment world was dominated by a single idea of risk, beautifully encapsulated in one number: beta. Beta told you how much a stock tended to move in relation to the overall market. If the market was the ocean, beta was a measure of how high your little boat would rise and fall with the tides. It was a revolutionary concept, but it's like trying to navigate a complex sea with only a compass. You know your general direction, but you're blind to the currents, the wind, and the hidden reefs.

Considering multiple risk dimensions is like upgrading from that simple compass to a full suite of modern navigational tools. It gives investors a richer, more complete map of the financial landscape, and the benefits are immense.

Why a Single Dimension Isn't Enough

Relying solely on market beta assumes that the only risk that matters is the systematic risk of the entire market. But reality is far more complex. The returns of an airline stock, for example, aren't just sensitive to the S&P 500. They are profoundly sensitive to oil prices. The returns of a bank are deeply tied to interest rate movements. A luxury goods company might be highly exposed to changes in consumer sentiment or currency exchange rates.

These are all distinct "risk dimensions" or factors. Ignoring them is like ignoring a hurricane warning just because the tide chart looks normal. By considering multiple risk dimensions, investors gain several key advantages:

Superior Risk Management: This is the most immediate benefit. A multi-dimensional view prevents you from being blindsided. You might have a portfolio with a low market beta, making you feel safe. However, a multifactor analysis could reveal that all your "safe" stocks are incredibly sensitive to inflation. If an unexpected inflation report comes out, your supposedly low-risk portfolio could suffer significant losses. By understanding your exposure to various factors—inflation, interest rates, credit spreads, commodity prices—you can hedge these risks or rebalance your portfolio to be less vulnerable. It's about ensuring there are no unpleasant surprises lurking beneath the surface.

More Accurate Performance Evaluation: Let's say a fund manager specializing in energy stocks has a fantastic year. A simple, single-factor model might show a huge alpha, suggesting genius stock-picking. But what if oil prices doubled that year? A multifactor model that includes an energy price factor would likely show that most of the manager's outperformance came from simply being exposed to rising oil prices—a factor exposure, not necessarily skill. This allows investors to properly distinguish between managers who are truly skilled and those who just got lucky by being in the right place at the right time. You pay managers for alpha, not for factor beta you could have gotten yourself more cheaply.

Enhanced Portfolio Customization: Every investor is different. Some might be retirees who are terrified of inflation eroding their fixed income. Others might be young entrepreneurs who believe in the long-term growth of small, innovative companies. Multifactor investing allows for the creation of highly tailored portfolios. An investor worried about inflation can build a portfolio with positive sensitivity to an inflation factor. An investor wanting to bet on the "value" premium can construct a portfolio tilted towards stocks with strong value characteristics. It moves beyond a one-size-fits-all approach to something that truly reflects an individual's views, goals, and risk tolerances.

Identification of New Opportunities: Thinking in multiple dimensions opens up new ways to generate returns. Instead of just betting on the market going up, investors can take positions on factors themselves. For example, if you believe that high-quality, stable companies are currently undervalued, you could build a portfolio that is long on a "quality" factor and short on a "low-quality" or "junk" factor. This is the foundation of many sophisticated investment strategies, allowing investors to isolate specific return drivers they have confidence in, without having to take on broad market risk. It's about finding new, uncorrelated sources of return that can make a portfolio more resilient over time.

In essence, moving from a single dimension to multiple dimensions of risk is a leap from a black-and-white photograph to a high-definition color movie. It provides depth, context, and a much more realistic view of the complex forces that shape investment returns, empowering investors to make smarter, more informed decisions.

Active Management: Deconstructing Risk and Measuring Skill

When you hire an active portfolio manager, you're not paying them to simply match the performance of a market index like the S&P 500. You can get that for a very low cost with an index fund. You're hiring them to beat the index. This deliberate deviation from the benchmark is the heart of active management, and it introduces a unique set of concepts: active risk, tracking risk, and the information ratio. Together, these metrics help us understand and evaluate a manager's strategy and skill.

The Sources of Active Risk

Active risk is the risk a manager takes on relative to their benchmark. It's a measure of how different the manager's portfolio is from the index they are trying to beat. If a manager's portfolio perfectly mirrors the S&P 500, their active risk is zero. But then, their returns will also perfectly mirror the index, and there's no chance of outperformance. To generate "alpha" (excess returns), a manager must take on active risk.

This risk doesn't just appear out of thin air. It stems from two fundamental sources:

Active Factor Tilts: This happens when a manager deliberately overweights or underweights certain systematic factors relative to the benchmark. For example, the benchmark index might have 20% exposure to technology stocks. An active manager who is bullish on tech might allocate 35% of their portfolio to that sector. This is an active bet. Similarly, a manager might decide to favor value stocks over growth stocks, or small-cap stocks over large-cap stocks, even if the benchmark is more balanced. Each of these "tilts" away from the benchmark's factor exposures is a source of active risk. The manager is essentially saying, "I believe these factors will outperform, and I'm positioning my portfolio to benefit."

Security Selection (Idiosyncratic Risk): This is the classic form of stock-picking. Within the technology sector, the benchmark might hold shares of Apple, Microsoft, and Google. The active manager might decide to overweight Apple, underweight Google, and completely avoid Microsoft. This decision to deviate from the benchmark's specific holdings introduces active risk. The manager is betting that their specific choices within a factor or sector will outperform the benchmark's choices. This is the risk that is unique to the specific assets chosen and is not explained by broad market factors.

Think of it like a chef trying to create a better version of a classic recipe (the benchmark). They might change the ingredient proportions (active factor tilts) or swap out a generic brand of chocolate for a specific artisanal one (security selection). Both decisions introduce the risk that their version might not taste better, but they are also the only way to potentially create something superior.

Interpreting Tracking Risk and the Information Ratio
So, we know a manager takes on active risk. But how do we measure it and judge if it's worth it? That's where tracking risk and the information ratio come in.

Tracking Risk (or Tracking Error)
Tracking risk is the standard deviation of the portfolio's active returns (the difference between the portfolio's return and the benchmark's return). In simpler terms, it quantifies how volatile your manager's performance is relative to the benchmark.

A low tracking risk (e.g., 1-2%) means the manager stays very close to the benchmark. Their returns won't deviate much, either on the upside or the downside. This is a "closet indexer." You can expect a very predictable, index-like journey.

A high tracking risk (e.g., 8-10%) means the manager is taking big bets. Their portfolio looks very different from the benchmark. This creates the potential for huge outperformance, but also the potential for massive underperformance. The journey will be much bumpier and less predictable.

Tracking risk itself isn't good or bad. It's a measure of how "active" the manager truly is. It tells you the magnitude of the bet being taken. The crucial follow-up question is: "Is the manager being rewarded for taking that risk?"

The Information Ratio (IR)
This is where it all comes together. The Information Ratio is perhaps the single most important metric for evaluating an active manager's skill. It tells you how much active return the manager has generated for each unit of active risk they have taken.

Interpreting the IR:

An IR of 0.5 is generally considered good. It means that for every 1% of tracking risk the manager took, they generated 0.5% of outperformance.

An IR of 1.0 is exceptional and very rare to sustain over long periods.

A negative IR is a disaster. It means the manager took on active risk (the portfolio was bumpy relative to the index) and still managed to underperform the benchmark. They were paid to take risks, and those risks didn't pay off.

The IR is the ultimate arbiter of skill. A manager who generates a 5% active return with a 5% tracking risk (IR = 1.0) is far more skilled than a manager who generates the same 5% active return but with a 10% tracking risk (IR = 0.5). The first manager was much more efficient and consistent in their risk-taking. The IR, therefore, helps us look past the simple headline return and understand the quality and consistency of the process that generated it.

Measuring and Managing Market Risk

The Role of Value at Risk (VaR) in Portfolio Risk Measurement

Imagine you're steering a large ship across the ocean. You need to know more than just your average speed; you need to understand the worst-case scenarios. What's the biggest wave you might realistically face? How much could you be thrown off course by a sudden storm? In the world of finance, Value at Risk (VaR) is like a weather forecast for your investment portfolio, giving you a single, concise number that estimates your potential losses. It doesn't predict the future with certainty, but it provides a crucial piece of information about the risks you're taking.

At its core, VaR answers a straightforward question: "What is the maximum amount of money I can expect to lose on my portfolio over a specific time period, at a certain level of confidence?"

Let's break down the three key ingredients of this question:

Maximum Loss: This is the "value" part of Value at Risk. It's a monetary figure, like $1 million, representing the potential downside.

Time Period: Risk is time-dependent. Are we talking about the risk over the next day, the next week, or the next month? A longer time horizon typically means a higher potential for loss. A common period for VaR calculation is one day or ten days.

Confidence Level: This is the probability part. Since we can't be 100% certain about the future, we set a confidence level, usually 95% or 99%. A 95% confidence level means that we can be 95% sure that our losses will not exceed the VaR amount. Conversely, it implies there is a 5% chance that our losses will be worse than the VaR estimate.

So, a VaR statement might look like this: "Our portfolio has a one-day VaR of $500,000 at a 99% confidence level." This simple sentence is packed with meaning. It tells the portfolio manager, the risk committee, and the investors that on any given day, there is a 99% probability that the portfolio will not lose more than $500,000. However, it also carries a warning: on one out of every 100 days, we can expect to lose more than $500,000. VaR helps quantify the risk of these "tail events"—the infrequent but potentially severe losses.

Why is VaR So Useful?
Before VaR became popular in the 1990s, risk was often discussed in complex, abstract terms using various statistical measures like standard deviation (volatility), beta, or delta. While useful for traders and analysts, these metrics are not very intuitive for senior management or investors who may not have a deep statistical background.

VaR's brilliance lies in its simplicity. It distills complex market movements and portfolio compositions into a single, easy-to-understand dollar amount. This has several powerful applications:

Risk Communication: It provides a common language for risk across different departments and levels of an organization. A CEO can understand a $10 million VaR figure much more readily than a portfolio beta of 1.2.

Risk Comparison: VaR allows for an apples-to-apples comparison of risk across different portfolios, asset classes, or even entire business units. A manager can see that their equities desk has a VaR of $2 million while the bond desk has a VaR of $750,000, providing a clear picture of where the firm's risk is concentrated.

Setting Risk Limits: Firms can set explicit VaR limits for traders and portfolio managers. If a trader's portfolio exceeds its assigned VaR limit, they must take action to reduce the risk, perhaps by selling some assets or hedging their positions. This acts as an essential control mechanism to prevent excessive risk-taking.

Performance Evaluation: When evaluating a manager's performance, just looking at their returns is not enough. A manager who generated a 20% return by taking massive risks might not be as skilled as one who generated a 15% return with much lower risk. By using risk-adjusted return metrics that incorporate VaR (like the Sharpe ratio), a firm can get a much better sense of a manager's true performance.

Regulatory Requirements: Following major financial crises, regulators have embraced VaR as a standard tool for capital adequacy. Banks are often required to hold a certain amount of capital in reserve, with the amount calculated based on their VaR. This ensures they have a sufficient buffer to absorb potential large losses without becoming insolvent.

However, VaR is not a silver bullet. It's a tool, and like any tool, it has limitations. A famous saying in finance is, "VaR tells you the most you can lose, if nothing goes wrong." The model's biggest weakness is that it doesn't tell you how much more you could lose on that unlucky 1% or 5% of days. The loss could be $500,001, or it could be $50 million. This "tail risk" is VaR's blind spot. Events like the 2008 financial crisis showed that these extreme, "black swan" events can and do happen, with losses far exceeding what VaR models might have suggested. For this reason, VaR is often used alongside other risk measures, like Stress Testing and Expected Shortfall, which specifically try to model the impact of these extreme negative events.

Comparing Methods for Estimating VaR

Calculating that single, powerful VaR number is not a simple task. There is no one "right" way to do it. The method chosen can significantly impact the final result and depends on the available data, the complexity of the portfolio, and the assumptions one is willing to make about the world. The three most widely used methods are the Parametric (Variance-Covariance), Historical Simulation, and Monte Carlo Simulation approaches. Each has a distinct philosophy, its own set of strengths, and its own unique blind spots.

1. The Parametric (Variance-Covariance) Method

The parametric method is the most traditional and, in many ways, the simplest approach. It gets its name because it relies on making a key assumption about the mathematical parameters of investment returns: it assumes that returns are normally distributed. Think of the classic bell curve you learned about in statistics. This method presumes that most daily returns will cluster around the average, and extreme gains or losses will be increasingly rare, following the smooth, predictable shape of that curve.

How it works:

To calculate VaR using this method, you need just two key statistical measures:

Expected Return (μ): The average return you expect from your portfolio.

Standard Deviation (σ): A measure of the portfolio's volatility, or how much its returns tend to swing around the average.

The VaR is then calculated using a simple formula: $VaR=[\mu-Z(\sigma)]\times PortfolioValue$, where 'Z' is the Z-score from the normal distribution that corresponds to your chosen confidence level (e.g., for 95% confidence, the Z-score is approximately 1.65).

Strengths:

Simplicity and Speed: Its primary advantage is that it's incredibly fast and easy to calculate, especially since you only need the mean and standard deviation. You don't need vast amounts of historical data.

Clear Formula: The calculation is transparent and easy to understand.

Weaknesses:

The Normality Assumption: This is its Achilles' heel. Financial markets are not perfectly normal. They are known for having "fat tails," meaning that extreme, crash-like events happen much more frequently than a perfect bell curve would predict. The parametric method systematically underestimates the risk of these tail events.

Doesn't Handle Options Well: This method struggles with portfolios containing non-linear instruments like options, whose price movements are not simple and direct.

Analogy: The parametric method is like assuming the weather will always be mild because the average yearly temperature is pleasant. It works fine most of the time, but it's completely unprepared for the sudden hurricane or blizzard that lies outside its "normal" assumptions.

2. The Historical Simulation Method

The historical simulation method takes a completely different, non-parametric approach. It throws out any assumptions about returns following a neat statistical distribution. Instead, it says, "The best guide to what might happen tomorrow is to look at what has actually happened in the past."

How it works:

This method is conceptually very simple. You gather a large dataset of the actual historical daily returns of your current portfolio over a long period (e.g., the last 500 days). To find the one-day 95% VaR, you simply line up these 500 past daily returns from worst to best. The VaR is then the loss that corresponds to the 5th percentile mark. For example, if you have 500 days of data, the 5th percentile would be the 25th worst day (500×0.05=25). The loss you experienced on that 25th worst day is your 95% VaR estimate.

Strengths:

No Assumptions: Its greatest strength is that it makes no assumptions about the distribution of returns. It directly uses real-world data, so it naturally captures the "fat tails," skewness, and any other weird quirks present in market history.

Easy to Understand and Implement: The logic is intuitive and easy to explain to non-specialists.

Handles All Assets: It can easily handle any type of financial instrument, including complex derivatives like options, because it just uses their actual historical price changes.

Weaknesses:

The Past is Not the Future: The method is entirely backward-looking. It implicitly assumes that the future will behave just like the recent past. If a new type of crisis occurs that has no precedent in your historical data set (like a global pandemic), the model will not see it coming.

Requires a Lot of Data: To be reliable, it needs a large and clean historical dataset, which may not always be available, especially for new assets.

Ghost Effects: A single, massive loss in the historical data (e.g., the 2008 crash) will keep the VaR high for years until that data point falls out of the observation window, at which point the VaR will suddenly drop, even if nothing in the current market has changed.

Analogy: The historical simulation is like a sea captain who navigates by only looking at the ship's wake. It gives a great idea of the waters you've just passed through but offers no insight into the iceberg that might be lurking just over the horizon.

3. The Monte Carlo Simulation Method 🎲
The Monte Carlo simulation is the most powerful, flexible, and computationally intensive of the three methods. It's a forward-looking approach that combines elements of the parametric method with the power of random simulation to explore a vast universe of possible futures.

How it works:
Instead of relying on history or a single distribution, this method starts by specifying statistical models for the risk

factors that drive the value of your portfolio (e.g., interest rates, stock prices, exchange rates). Then, it uses a computer to generate thousands, or even hundreds of thousands, of random potential future paths for these factors over the desired time horizon (e.g., one day). For each of these simulated future scenarios, the portfolio is re-valued, calculating a potential profit or loss.

The end result is a massive distribution of thousands of possible portfolio outcomes. Just like with the historical method, you then sort these outcomes from worst to best, and the 5th percentile of this simulated distribution becomes your 95% VaR.

Strengths:

Flexibility and Power: It can model virtually any kind of distribution and handle any complex, non-linear instrument with incredible accuracy. It allows you to model how different risks correlate and interact.

Forward-Looking: It's not constrained by historical events. You can program it to simulate scenarios that have never happened before, making it excellent for stress testing.

Overcomes Normality Issues: It can easily incorporate "fat-tailed" distributions that are more representative of real-world financial markets.

Weaknesses:

Model Risk: Its accuracy is entirely dependent on the quality of the statistical models and assumptions you feed into it. If your assumptions about how markets behave are wrong, the output will be meaningless ("garbage in, garbage out").

Computationally Expensive: Running tens of thousands of complex simulations requires significant computing power and time, making it the most resource-intensive method.

Complexity: It is a "black box" to many, making it difficult to explain and interpret without specialized knowledge.

Analogy: The Monte Carlo simulation is like using a sophisticated weather simulator. You input current atmospheric conditions and physical laws, and it runs thousands of virtual weather patterns to forecast the probability of a storm. Its accuracy depends entirely on how well your model captures the real physics of the atmosphere.

Value at Risk, or VaR, is a cornerstone of modern financial risk management. At its heart, it's a simple idea that tries to answer a straightforward question: "What's the most I can expect to lose on this investment over a specific time period, with a certain level of confidence?" It boils down the complex, multifaceted nature of financial risk into a single, digestible number. For example, a bank might state that its one-day 99% VaR is $10 million. This means that on any given day, there is only a 1% chance that the bank will lose more than $10 million. It's a probabilistic estimate of potential loss, a vital tool for executives, regulators, and investors trying to get a handle on the downside risk of their portfolios.

Estimating and Interpreting Value at Risk (VaR)
Calculating this single, powerful number isn't a one-size-fits-all process. The method you choose depends on the available data, the complexity of the portfolio, and the assumptions you're willing to make about the world. There are three primary methods used to estimate VaR: the Parametric method, the Historical Simulation method, and

the Monte Carlo Simulation method. Each offers a different lens through which to view potential risk.

The Parametric Method (Variance-Covariance)
Think of the parametric method as the "perfect world" approach to risk. It's the most straightforward of the three, relying heavily on some elegant but significant assumptions. The biggest assumption is that the returns of the assets in your portfolio follow a normal distribution—that classic, symmetrical bell curve you might remember from statistics. This assumption is powerful because if we know that returns are normally distributed, we can describe the entire range of possible outcomes using just two parameters: the expected return (the average) and the standard deviation (a measure of how spread out the returns are).

The process works like this:

Gather the Data: First, you need historical data for the assets in your portfolio to calculate their expected returns and standard deviations. Crucially, you also need to figure out the correlation between these assets—how they tend to move together. Do they rise and fall in unison, or does one zig when the other zags? This is captured in a variance-covariance matrix.

Calculate Portfolio Statistics: Using the weights of each asset in your portfolio, you combine their individual expected returns and standard deviations (along with their correlations) to calculate the overall expected return and standard deviation for the entire portfolio.

Choose a Confidence Level: This is the "certainty" part of the VaR question. Common levels are 95% or 99%. This choice determines a "Z-score" from the standard normal distribution. For a 95% confidence level, the Z-score is about 1.65, and for 99%, it's about 2.33. This score tells you how many standard deviations away from the average you need to go to capture 95% or 99% of all expected outcomes.

Calculate VaR: The final calculation is relatively simple. You use the formula:

VaR=[(Portfolio Expected Return)−Z×(Portfolio Standard Deviation)]×(Portfolio Value)
Interpreting the Result: Let's say you have a $100 million portfolio, and your one-day 95% parametric VaR comes out to be $1.5 million. The interpretation is: "Under the assumption of normal returns, we are 95% confident that our portfolio will not lose more than $1.5 million over the next trading day." It provides a clear, concise boundary for what is considered a "normal" market loss.

The beauty of the parametric method is its simplicity and speed. Once you have the statistical parameters, calculating VaR is quick. However, its greatest strength—the reliance on the normal distribution—is also its most significant weakness. Financial markets are famously not always "normal." They are prone to extreme, unexpected events (like market crashes) that happen far more frequently than a perfect bell curve would suggest. This phenomenon is known as "fat tails," and the parametric method can severely underestimate risk during turbulent times because it doesn't adequately account for these rare but devastating events.

The Historical Simulation Method
If the parametric method is the "perfect world" approach, the historical simulation method is the "show me the evidence" approach. It completely ditches the assumption of a normal distribution. Instead of trying to fit the data to a predefined mathematical curve, it lets the

past data speak for itself. It operates on a simple, intuitive premise: the future will probably look a lot like the past.

Here's how it unfolds:

Gather Historical Data: You collect a long history of daily price changes for all the assets in your current portfolio. For a one-day VaR, you might look at the last 250 trading days (about one year) or even 500 days.

Simulate Portfolio Returns: You then take this historical data and apply it to your current portfolio. For each day in your historical window (e.g., each of the last 250 days), you pretend that those historical market movements happened to your portfolio today. This gives you a list of 250 hypothetical daily profit-and-loss (P&L) scenarios for your current portfolio.

Rank the Outcomes: You take this list of 250 P&L outcomes and rank them from the worst loss to the highest gain.

Find the VaR: Finally, you simply look down the ranked list to find the loss that corresponds to your chosen confidence level. If you want a 95% VaR, you're looking for the point that separates the worst 5% of outcomes from the rest. With 250 data points, the 5% worst outcomes would be the 12.5 worst days (you'd typically round or interpolate). The VaR would be the loss on that 13th-worst day.

Interpreting the Result: If that 13th-worst day in your simulation resulted in a loss of $1.8 million, your interpretation is: "Based on market movements over the last 250 days, there is a 5% chance that our portfolio could lose $1.8 million or more in a single day."

The primary advantage of historical simulation is its simplicity and freedom from assumptions about the distribution of returns. It naturally captures the "fat tails" and weird correlations that really happen in markets because it's using actual historical data. However, it's not without its flaws. Its biggest limitation is its complete reliance on the past. It implicitly assumes that the volatility and correlations of the recent past are perfect guides for the immediate future. If a completely unprecedented event occurs—a "black swan"—the historical simulation will not see it coming, as it is not present in the historical data set. Furthermore, if the market was unusually calm during your historical window, the VaR estimate might be dangerously low.

The Monte Carlo Simulation Method

The Monte Carlo simulation method is the most powerful, flexible, and computationally intensive of the three. It's a "what if" machine that creates its own future. Instead of being confined to the assumptions of a normal distribution or the rigid path of history, Monte Carlo builds thousands of possible future scenarios from the ground up.

This is the process:

Model the Risk Factors: First, you need to choose a mathematical model that you believe accurately describes the behavior of the key risk factors affecting your portfolio (e.g., interest rates, stock prices, exchange rates). This is a critical step and requires significant expertise. For example, you might model stock prices using a process like geometric Brownian motion, which incorporates a drift (expected return) and a random "shock" (volatility).

Run Thousands of Simulations: Using powerful computers, you generate thousands (or even hundreds of thousands) of random paths for each risk factor based on the models you chose. Each complete set of paths represents one possible "future day."

Revalue the Portfolio: For each of these thousands of simulated future days, you calculate the value of your portfolio. This gives you a massive distribution of possible portfolio P&L outcomes.

Determine the VaR: Just like with the historical simulation, you rank all these simulated P&L outcomes from worst to best. You then find the percentile that corresponds to your confidence level. For a 99% VaR on 100,000 simulations, you would look at the 1,000th-worst outcome.

Interpreting the Result: If the 1,000th-worst outcome in your 100,000 simulations is a loss of $2.1 million, the interpretation is: "Based on our models of how markets behave, our simulations show a 1% probability that our portfolio will lose $2.1 million or more in the next day."

The great strength of Monte Carlo is its incredible flexibility. It can handle a vast array of complex, non-linear instruments (like options) and can incorporate any distribution or market behavior you can model, including fat tails or sudden volatility spikes. It's not constrained by history. However, it has its own set of challenges. The results are only as good as the models you put in—a concept known as "GIGO" (Garbage In, Garbage Out). If your assumptions about how stock prices or interest rates behave are wrong, your VaR estimate will be wrong. It is also extremely demanding on computer resources and can be slow to run, making it less suitable for real-time risk calculations.

Advantages and Limitations of VaR

While VaR is an incredibly useful tool, it's essential to have a clear-eyed view of both what it does well and where it falls short. A misunderstanding of its limitations can lead to a dangerous false sense of security.

Advantages of VaR

The widespread adoption of VaR across the financial industry is a testament to its compelling benefits.

A Single, Simple Metric: Perhaps its greatest advantage is its ability to distill complex, hard-to-understand market risks into a single monetary value. It's far easier for a company's board of directors to grasp the statement "Our one-day 99% VaR is $5 million" than to digest a complicated report on standard deviations, correlations, and option greeks. This simplicity facilitates communication about risk across all levels of an organization, from the trading floor to the C-suite.

A Universal Benchmark: VaR provides a common framework for measuring risk. It allows a firm to compare the risk of a foreign exchange trading desk with that of a government bond portfolio in a consistent, apples-to-apples manner. This standardization helps in making informed decisions about capital allocation. If two different business units are generating similar profits but one has a significantly higher VaR, management can allocate capital more efficiently to the unit that produces better risk-adjusted returns.

Performance Evaluation: By measuring risk in a standardized way, VaR allows for better performance evaluation. A trader who generates a $20 million profit might seem like a star, but if they did so while taking on a level of risk represented by a $15 million VaR, their performance is very different from another trader who made $18 million with a VaR of only $4 million. It adds a crucial layer of context to raw profit numbers.

Setting Risk Limits: VaR is a practical tool for risk management. A firm can set explicit VaR limits for individual traders, desks, or the entire organization. If a trader's portfolio exceeds its VaR limit, it triggers an immediate review, forcing a reduction in the position or a re-evaluation of the strategy before potential losses can spiral out of control.

Regulatory Acceptance: For better or worse, VaR has become an industry and regulatory standard. Frameworks like the Basel Accords, which set international banking standards, require banks to calculate VaR to determine the amount of capital they must hold in reserve to cushion against financial distress. This makes VaR not just a good idea, but a necessity for many financial institutions.

Limitations of VaR

Despite its benefits, VaR has significant blind spots that can be perilous if ignored. The 2008 financial crisis highlighted many of these weaknesses in dramatic fashion.

VaR is Not the Maximum Possible Loss: This is the single most important and most frequently misunderstood limitation. VaR tells you the minimum loss you can expect on a bad day, not the maximum. A 99% VaR of $10 million means that 1% of the time, you should expect to lose more than $10 million. It tells you nothing about whether that loss will be $10.1 million or $100 million. It defines the boundary of "normal" days but is silent about the magnitude of the disaster that lies beyond it. Financial author Nassim Taleb famously criticized it, comparing it to an airbag that works perfectly in every situation except when you have a crash.

False Sense of Security: The deceptive simplicity of VaR can lull executives into a false sense of security. A single number can make risk seem manageable and precisely quantifiable. This can lead to complacency and a failure to prepare for the extreme "tail events" that VaR doesn't measure. Believing you have a handle on risk because you have a VaR number can be more dangerous than admitting you don't know the full extent of your exposure.

Sensitivity to Assumptions and Inputs: As discussed with the estimation methods, the VaR number is highly dependent on the inputs and assumptions used. The parametric method relies on a normal distribution, which is often unrealistic. The historical method assumes the future will resemble the past, which is not always true. Monte Carlo simulations are only as good as the models they are built on. Different methods can produce vastly different VaR figures for the same portfolio, making the "true" risk hard to pin down.

It Doesn't Capture All Risks: VaR is primarily a measure of market risk—the risk of losses from changes in prices, interest rates, etc. It does not inherently capture other critical types of risk. For example, it doesn't measure liquidity risk. Your VaR might be $2 million, but if a crisis hits and you can't sell your assets at all without causing a massive price drop, your actual loss could be far greater. It also doesn't capture credit risk (the risk of a counterparty defaulting) or operational risk (the risk of losses from failed internal processes or fraud).

It Can Discourage Diversification (Subadditivity): A properly behaved risk measure should be "subadditive," meaning the risk of two portfolios combined should be less than or equal to the sum of their individual risks. VaR sometimes violates this principle. It is possible to combine two portfolios and have the VaR of the new, combined portfolio be greater than the sum of the VaRs of the individual portfolios. This can create perverse incentives, discouraging sensible diversification. To address this and other limitations, alternative risk measures like Expected Shortfall (ES) or Conditional VaR (CVaR) have been developed. ES attempts to answer the question, "If things go bad, how bad do we expect them to be?" by averaging all the losses in the tail beyond the VaR point.

Extensions of VaR: Looking Beyond the Single Number Value at Risk, or VaR, is a cornerstone of financial risk management. It gives us a single, neat number that answers a crucial question: "What's the most I can expect to lose on this investment over a specific time period, with a certain level of confidence?" For example, a 1-day 99% VaR of $1 million means there's a 99% chance you won't lose more than $1 million by tomorrow. It's a fantastic starting point, a simple snapshot of potential downside. But like any snapshot, it doesn't tell the whole story. What about that other 1%? What happens in the absolute worst-case scenarios? And how does one part of my portfolio affect the risk of the whole thing? This is where the extensions of VaR come into play, adding depth and color to that black-and-white picture.

One of the most important extensions is Conditional VaR (CVaR), also known as Expected Shortfall (ES). Think of it as VaR's more cautious and insightful older sibling. While VaR tells you the threshold of a bad loss, CVaR tells you the average loss you can expect if you actually cross that threshold. It answers the question, "If things go really bad, just how bad could it get on average?" Let's go back to our $1 million VaR. VaR stops there; it draws a line in the sand. CVaR, on the other hand, peeks over that line and calculates the average of all the losses that are even worse than $1 million. This is incredibly useful because two portfolios can have the same VaR but wildly different

CVaRs. One might have a small chance of a loss just slightly over $1 million, while the other might have a small chance of a catastrophic, company-ending loss. CVaR captures this "tail risk," giving a much fuller picture of the potential for extreme pain. It helps us understand the severity of our worst days, not just their starting point.

Then we have Marginal VaR (MVaR). This clever tool helps us understand how adding a new position to our portfolio changes the overall risk. Imagine you're a portfolio manager, and you're considering buying a new stock. MVaR calculates the rate of change in the total portfolio VaR as you add a tiny bit more of that new stock. It essentially isolates the risk contribution of that specific position at the margin. Is this new asset a diversifier that will reduce your overall VaR, or is it a risk concentrator that will send it soaring? MVaR gives you the answer. It's like a risk-o-meter for every dollar you're thinking of investing, telling you the immediate impact on your portfolio's total VaR. This is vital for optimizing a portfolio, allowing managers to fine-tune their holdings by understanding the marginal risk impact of each component.

Closely related is Incremental VaR (IVaR). While Marginal VaR is about the rate of change from a tiny addition, Incremental VaR measures the exact change in portfolio VaR that comes from adding or subtracting a specific position. It's not a rate of change; it's the actual dollar amount of VaR that a particular trade will add or remove. For instance, if you want to know precisely how much your portfolio's VaR will change by adding $5 million worth of Apple stock, IVaR is your go-to measure. It's a practical, before-and-after calculation. This makes it an indispensable tool for traders and risk managers evaluating the real-world impact of their decisions. Should we make this trade? IVaR helps to provide a concrete, risk-based answer. These extensions transform VaR from a simple warning light into a sophisticated diagnostic toolkit, allowing for a much more nuanced and robust approach to managing financial risk.

The Risk Manager's Toolkit: Sensitivity, Scenarios, and VaR
Imagine you're navigating a ship. You'd want to know more than just the probability of hitting a rock (which is what VaR sort of tells you). You'd also want to know how sensitive your ship is to the turning of the rudder and what would happen if a massive, unexpected storm suddenly appeared. In finance, sensitivity risk measures are like understanding your ship's rudder, while scenario risk measures are like running drills for that giant storm. They work alongside VaR to provide a comprehensive view of the risks you face.

Sensitivity risk measures are all about the "what if" questions on a small scale. They measure how much the value of your investment will change in response to a small change in a specific market factor, like an interest rate or a stock price. They are the fine-tuning instruments in a risk manager's toolkit. For the world of bonds and fixed-income, the most famous sensitivity measure is duration. Duration tells you approximately how much a bond's price will fall if interest rates rise by 1%. A bond with a higher duration is more sensitive to interest rate changes, like a ship that turns sharply with even a small touch of the rudder. In the world of options, we have the "Greeks." Delta, for example, measures how much an option's price will change for every $1 move in the underlying stock's price. These measures are precise, elegant, and incredibly useful for day-to-day hedging and risk management. They tell you where your specific vulnerabilities are.

On the other hand, scenario risk measures are about the big picture and the giant "what ifs." Instead of looking at a tiny change in one variable, scenario analysis involves building a plausible, large-scale story about the future and seeing how your portfolio holds up. This could be a historical scenario, like re-living the 2008 financial crisis, or a hypothetical one, like "What if oil prices triple and inflation hits 10%?" You model this entire economic storm and calculate the resulting profit or loss on your portfolio. This isn't about small, precise adjustments; it's about stress testing your entire strategy against a major market event. It helps you find hidden correlations and vulnerabilities that sensitivity measures might miss. It answers the question, "Can my portfolio survive a nightmare?"

So, how do these compare to VaR? The three approaches are more like complementary partners than competitors.

Perspective: VaR is a probabilistic measure. It looks at the normal, day-to-day fluctuations of the market and tells you the boundary of expected losses based on historical data. Sensitivity measures are localized and deterministic; they tell you exactly what happens if one specific factor moves a little. Scenario analysis is holistic and deterministic; it looks at a big, specific event and calculates the impact.

The Question They Answer: VaR answers, "How bad can it get under normal conditions?" Sensitivity measures answer, "How reactive is my portfolio to small changes in key factors?" Scenario analysis answers, "What happens to my portfolio if this specific, major event occurs?"

Strengths & Weaknesses: VaR's strength is its simplicity—a single number that summarizes overall market risk. Its weakness is that it says nothing about what happens beyond its threshold (the "tail risk") and can be misleading if historical data isn't a good guide for the future. Sensitivity measures are great for precise hedging but can fail during a crisis when all the usual relationships between market factors break down. Scenario analysis is brilliant for exploring extreme events and understanding complex interactions, but its weakness is that it's only as good as the scenarios you can imagine, and it doesn't tell you how likely those scenarios are to happen.

In essence, a good risk manager uses all three. They use VaR to get a daily, high-level snapshot of risk. They use sensitivity measures to manage and hedge their specific exposures. And they use scenario analysis to prepare for the storms they hope will never come.

Managing the Market's Mood: Taming Risk in Equities, Bonds, and Options

Every type of financial asset dances to its own rhythm, reacting differently to the market's ever-changing mood. Managing market risk—the risk of losses from factors that affect the entire market—and volatility risk—the risk from changes in the size of market swings—requires specific tools for each asset class. It's about understanding and controlling your exposure to these broad forces. Let's look at how this is done for equities, fixed-income, and options.

Equities and Beta

For equities (stocks), the king of exposure measures is Beta (β). Beta measures a stock's volatility, or systematic risk, in relation to the overall market (like the S&P 500).

A Beta of 1 means the stock moves in line with the market. If the market goes up 10%, the stock tends to go up 10%.

A Beta greater than 1 indicates the stock is more volatile than the market. A stock with a Beta of 1.5 would be expected to rise 15% if the market rises 10%, but it would also fall 15% if the market falls 10%. These are your high-growth tech stocks or cyclical companies.

A Beta less than 1 suggests the stock is less volatile. Utility or consumer staples stocks often have low Betas.

A Beta of 0 means the stock's movement is completely uncorrelated with the market (like a Treasury bill).

How is this used? A portfolio manager can actively manage their market risk by adjusting the overall Beta of their portfolio. If they are feeling bullish and expect the market to rise, they might "increase the Beta" of their portfolio by buying more high-Beta stocks. This amplifies their potential gains. Conversely, if they fear a market downturn, they can lower the portfolio's Beta by shifting into less volatile, low-Beta stocks or even shorting high-Beta stocks to protect against losses. Beta provides a simple, powerful lever to control the portfolio's sensitivity to broad market movements.

Fixed-Income: Duration and Convexity
For fixed-income (bonds), the primary source of market risk is changes in interest rates. The main tools here are duration and convexity. As we mentioned earlier, duration is a measure of a bond's price sensitivity to interest rate changes. A portfolio manager who expects interest rates to fall (and bond prices to rise) might extend the duration of their portfolio by buying longer-term bonds. If they expect rates to rise, they would shorten the portfolio's duration to minimize the potential price drop.

But duration is a linear approximation; it works well for small interest rate changes but becomes less accurate for larger ones. This is where convexity comes in. Convexity measures the curvature in the relationship between bond prices and interest rates. A portfolio with positive convexity will have better performance than duration alone would suggest, whether rates rise or fall. It's a kind of "risk buffer." Managers actively seek to build portfolios with positive convexity. By managing both duration and convexity, a bond portfolio manager can precisely position their holdings to profit from their interest rate forecasts while simultaneously building in a buffer against inaccurate predictions.

Options and the "Greeks"

Options are in a league of their own because their value is sensitive to many factors at once. To manage this, traders use a set of sensitivity measures known as the "Greeks."

Delta: Measures sensitivity to the price of the underlying asset. It's the key tool for hedging directional market risk. A "delta-neutral" portfolio is one that is, for a moment, immune to small moves in the underlying market price.

Gamma: Measures the rate of change of Delta. It's a measure of second-order risk. Managing gamma is crucial because a delta-neutral position can quickly become unhedged if the market moves significantly.

Vega: This is the big one for managing volatility risk. Vega measures how much an option's price changes for every 1% change in the implied volatility of the underlying asset. If a trader believes volatility is about to spike, they can construct a "long vega" position (by buying options) to profit from that increase in market choppiness. If they think volatility will decrease, they can create a "short vega" position. Vega allows traders to make direct bets on and hedge against changes in the market's "fear gauge."

Theta: Measures sensitivity to the passage of time (time decay).

By balancing these Greeks, an options trader can isolate and manage their risks with incredible precision. They can set up a portfolio that is neutral to market direction (delta-neutral) but designed to profit from an explosion in volatility (long vega), effectively separating and managing market risk and volatility risk as two distinct exposures. This demonstrates the sophisticated ways modern finance provides tools not just to measure risk, but to actively shape and manage it.

The Tools of the Trade: Sensitivity and Scenario Risk Measures

Imagine you're the captain of a ship. You wouldn't set sail without knowing how your vessel reacts to different sea conditions, right? You'd want to know how much it might tilt if a strong wind hits its sails or how it would handle a giant wave. In the world of finance, managing a portfolio of investments is a lot like captaining that ship, and the "sea conditions" are the constantly shifting market factors like interest rates, stock prices, and currency exchange rates. To navigate these turbulent waters, portfolio managers and risk analysts use special tools called risk measures. Two of the most fundamental types are sensitivity risk measures and scenario risk measures.

Think of sensitivity risk measures as the ship's manual for small, predictable changes. They answer the question: "If one specific thing changes by a tiny amount, how much does my portfolio's value wobble?" These measures are incredibly focused. They isolate a single market factor—like a one-percent change in interest rates—and calculate the immediate impact on your investments. It's like gently pushing the ship's rudder to see how quickly it turns. You're not trying to simulate a hurricane; you're just testing its responsiveness.

Some of the most common sensitivity measures have specific names that you might hear finance professionals throw around. For bonds, a key measure is duration. In simple terms, duration tells you how much a bond's price is likely to change if interest rates move by 1%. A bond with a higher duration is like a ship with a very large sail; even a small gust of wind (a small change in interest rates) can cause a big change in its path (its price). Another one for bonds is convexity, which fine-tunes the estimate provided by duration, accounting for the fact that the relationship between bond prices and interest rates isn't perfectly linear.

For stocks and stock options, you'll hear about the "Greeks." The most famous is delta, which measures how much an option's price will change for every $1 move in the underlying stock's price. If an option has a delta of 0.50, its price will go up by about 50 cents if the stock price rises by a dollar. Other Greeks like gamma (measuring the rate of change of delta) and vega (measuring sensitivity to volatility) provide even more nuanced insights. At their core, all these sensitivity measures do the same thing: they provide a quick, clean snapshot of how a portfolio reacts to a small, isolated market nudge. They are the essential, everyday instruments on the captain's dashboard.

On the other hand, scenario risk measures are the ship's emergency drills. They don't bother with small, gentle nudges. Instead, they ask the big, scary "what if" questions. What if a massive storm hits? What if the engine fails in the middle of the ocean? In financial terms, this translates to: "What would happen to my portfolio's value if a major, complex market event occurred?" Instead of changing just one variable, a scenario analysis involves changing many variables all at once to simulate a specific, plausible future event.

These events can be based on history or imagination. A historical scenario might replay a past crisis, like the 2008 global financial crisis or the tech bubble bursting in 2000. A risk manager would apply the exact market movements that happened during that period—stock market crashes, interest rate spikes, currency collapses—to their current portfolio to see how much money they would have lost. It's like putting the ship through a simulation of a famous historical hurricane to see if it would have survived.

A hypothetical scenario, however, is forward-looking and more creative. It's based on plausible future events that haven't happened yet. For example, a risk manager might model the impact of a sudden escalation in a trade war, a major sovereign debt default in Europe, or a surprisingly sharp increase in inflation that forces central banks to raise interest rates aggressively. These scenarios are carefully constructed stories about the future, with all the interconnected market movements fleshed out. The goal isn't to predict the future with certainty, but to understand the portfolio's potential vulnerabilities under extreme stress. This is often called stress testing. By running these fire drills, the captain can identify the weakest points in the ship's structure before the real storm arrives, allowing them to reinforce them ahead of time.

Weighing the Pros and Cons: A Look at the Measures' Strengths and Weaknesses

Every tool has its purpose, and it's just as important to know what a tool can't do as it is to know what it can. Sensitivity and scenario measures are no different; they each come with a distinct set of advantages and limitations that make them suitable for different tasks. Understanding this trade-off is crucial for any risk manager trying to build a complete picture of the dangers they face.

Let's start with sensitivity measures. Their biggest advantage is their simplicity and ease of calculation. Measures like duration and delta are often straightforward to compute and can be boiled down to a single, easy-to-understand number. This makes them incredibly useful for day-to-day risk monitoring. A trader can see the delta of their options book at a glance and know their immediate exposure to small price moves in the underlying stock. This allows for quick, tactical adjustments. They provide a clear, standardized language for risk. When one manager talks about a portfolio's duration, another manager instantly understands the interest rate sensitivity being described. This makes it easy to aggregate risks across different desks, departments, and even entire firms. They provide a precise answer to a very specific question, which is perfect for hedging and fine-tuning a portfolio's risk profile.

However, this laser focus is also their greatest weakness. Sensitivity measures operate under the assumption that only one thing changes at a time, while everything else stays constant—a condition that almost never happens in the real world. Markets are messy and interconnected. A jump in oil prices doesn't just affect oil stocks; it affects inflation, which affects interest rates, which affects bond prices and currency values. Sensitivity measures miss these crucial correlations. They are also fundamentally linear approximations. They work well for small changes but can be wildly inaccurate for large, sudden market moves. Duration might tell you what happens if rates move by 0.1%, but it's a poor guide for what happens if they jump by 3% overnight. They can create a false sense of security by ignoring the "non-linear" risks—the sudden, explosive breaks from the norm where the real damage happens. In short, they are great for measuring ripples but terrible for measuring tsunamis.

Now, let's turn to scenario measures. Their primary advantage is their ability to capture the complexity and interconnectedness of real-world market events. When you simulate a financial crisis, you're not just shocking one variable; you're moving interest rates, stock prices, credit spreads, and liquidity conditions all at once, just as they would move in a real panic. This provides a much more holistic and intuitive picture of what a portfolio's losses could look like during a period of major stress. They help answer the big-picture questions about survival, not just minor fluctuations. This makes them invaluable for stress testing and understanding tail risk—the risk of rare but catastrophic events. By forcing managers to think about extreme but plausible futures, scenario analysis can reveal hidden vulnerabilities that sensitivity measures would completely miss. For example, it might show that while a portfolio is hedged against small interest rate moves, it would suffer massive losses in a "flight to quality" scenario where correlations change dramatically. They are powerful tools for communication with senior management and regulators because they tell a story that is easy to grasp: "If this event happens, this is how much we could lose."

The limitations of scenario analysis, however, are significant. The biggest one is that the analysis is only as good as the scenarios you choose. You might run a dozen detailed scenarios, but if the next crisis looks completely different from all of them, your analysis won't have prepared you. There's a real danger of "fighting the last war" by focusing too much on historical scenarios. The future is rarely a perfect repeat of the past. Furthermore, designing these scenarios can be highly subjective and complex. Deciding how different market variables will interact during a hypothetical crisis requires a lot of assumptions and expert judgment, and different analysts can come to very different conclusions. Finally, scenario analysis doesn't tell you anything about the probability of the event occurring. It might show a potential billion-dollar loss in a severe recession scenario, but it doesn't quantify whether that scenario has a 1% chance of happening next year or a 0.01% chance. This makes it difficult to use for setting precise risk limits or calculating the expected cost of risk over time.

Setting the Boundaries: How Firms Control Market Risk

Knowing your risks is one thing, but actively managing and controlling them is another. A firm can't simply calculate its sensitivities and run stress tests and then hope for the best. It needs to establish clear rules and boundaries to ensure that its risk-takers don't expose the entire organization to catastrophic losses. These rules are known as risk limits or constraints. They are the guardrails on the highway of financial markets, designed to keep traders and portfolio managers from steering off a cliff. Let's explore some of the most common constraints used to manage market risk.

Risk Budgeting

At the highest level, a firm uses risk budgeting. Think of this like a financial budget, but instead of allocating dollars, the firm's leadership allocates a "budget" of acceptable risk to different business units, trading desks, or portfolio managers. This risk is often measured using a sophisticated statistical metric like Value-at-Risk (VaR), which estimates the maximum potential loss over a specific time period at a certain confidence level (e.g., "we are 99% confident we won't lose more than $10 million in a single day"). The total risk budget for the firm is determined by its overall risk appetite—how much of a loss it's willing and able to absorb. This total budget is then cascaded down. The equities division might get a $4 million VaR budget, the bond trading desk gets $3 million, and so on. This approach ensures that risk-taking is aligned with the firm's strategic goals and that no single part of the business can consume a disproportionate amount of the firm's total capacity for risk. It's a top-down way to make sure everyone is on the same page.

Position Limits

While risk budgeting is a great top-down approach, firms also need more granular, bottom-up controls. This is where position limits come in. These are simple, direct rules that restrict the size of a position a trader can take in a specific security or asset class. A position limit might be stated in absolute terms (e.g., "no more than $20 million invested in the stock of any single company" or "you cannot hold more than 500,000 barrels of crude oil"). It could also be set as a percentage of the total portfolio or as a percentage of the market's daily trading volume to prevent a single firm from dominating a market and causing liquidity problems. The primary goal of position limits is to ensure diversification and prevent excessive concentration in one single bet. Even if a trader's overall risk budget (measured by VaR) is within its limit, a massive, concentrated position could still be incredibly dangerous if that one specific company or commodity experiences a sudden, catastrophic event that VaR models might not capture. Position limits are a blunt but highly effective safety net.

Scenario Limits

Tying back to our earlier discussion, firms also use the outputs of scenario analysis to set limits. A scenario limit specifies the maximum acceptable loss that a portfolio or desk is allowed to show under a particular, predefined stress scenario. For example, the firm's risk committee might decree that the emerging markets desk cannot lose more than $50 million in a "Repeat of the 1997 Asian Financial Crisis" scenario. This forces the desk's manager to structure their portfolio not just to manage day-to-day risk, but also to be resilient to specific types of systemic shocks. These limits are crucial because they address the weaknesses of other measures. While a portfolio's VaR might look perfectly acceptable, a scenario limit can highlight a hidden vulnerability to a specific type of market crash where correlations break down. It forces managers to think beyond the normal statistical distributions and prepare for the storm, not just the rain.

Stop-Loss Limits

Finally, we have stop-loss limits. These are arguably the most straightforward and reactive type of risk control. A stop-loss limit is a pre-determined level of loss at which a position must be automatically closed out, no questions asked. It's a circuit breaker designed to cap the damage from a losing trade before it spirals out of control. For example, a trader might buy a stock at $100 with a stop-loss limit of 10%. If the stock price falls to $90, the position is automatically sold. This enforces discipline and takes the emotion out of the decision to cut losses. Without such a rule, a trader might be tempted to "hold on and hope," turning a small, manageable loss into a devastating one. Stop-loss limits can be set on an individual position, a trader's entire portfolio, or even a whole desk. They are the ultimate backstop, ensuring that when a bet goes wrong, the bleeding is stopped quickly.

Capital Allocation: Steering the Ship with Risk Measures

Imagine you're the captain of a large shipping company. You have a fleet of ships (your business units) and a certain amount of fuel (your capital). You can't just give all the fuel to the biggest ship or the one that shouts the loudest. You need a smart way to decide how much fuel each ship gets to maximize the company's profit while ensuring no ship runs out of fuel mid-journey, especially if a storm hits. This, in essence, is the challenge of capital allocation.

In the world of finance, capital allocation is the process of distributing a firm's financial resources, its capital, among its various business lines, projects, or investments. The goal isn't just to fund everything; it's to do so intelligently to get the best bang for your buck, or what we call the best risk-adjusted return. Just throwing money at the most profitable division might seem tempting, but what if that division is also incredibly risky, like a ship sailing straight into a known hurricane zone? That's where risk measures come in. They are the captain's advanced weather reports and navigation charts. They help quantify the potential "storms" each business unit might face, allowing the firm to allocate capital not just based on potential rewards, but also on the potential for disaster.

The Role of Risk-Adjusted Performance
The core idea is to create a level playing field. It's not fair to compare the raw profit of a very safe, stable business unit (like a tugboat operating in a calm harbor) with that of a high-risk, high-return one (like an exploratory vessel in the Arctic). We need a metric that accounts for the risk taken to achieve a profit. This is where Risk-Adjusted Return on Capital (RAROC) becomes the star of the show.

Let's break that down. Expected Return is the profit we anticipate a business unit will generate. That's the easy part. The magic happens in the denominator: Economic Capital.

Economic Capital is not the same as the regulatory capital that a bank is required to hold by law. Instead, it's the amount of money the firm itself calculates it needs to have in reserve to absorb unexpected losses over a certain period, with a certain level of confidence. Think of it as the firm's own internal "rainy day fund" for a truly catastrophic storm. If a business unit is very risky, it will require a larger slice of this economic capital. It's like telling the captain of the Arctic vessel, "Your journey is dangerous, so you need to carry more emergency supplies (capital) than the tugboat."

By dividing the return by the risk (economic capital), RAROC gives us a single, powerful number. A business unit with a high RAROC is generating a lot of profit for the amount of risk it's taking on. A unit with a low RAROC might be profitable, but it's chewing up a disproportionate amount of the firm's risk capacity to do so.

How It Works in Practice

So, how does a company use this?

Decision Making: The firm sets a minimum acceptable RAROC, a "hurdle rate." Any new project or existing business line that can't meet this rate is either rejected, repriced, or restructured. If an investment promises a $1 million return but requires $20 million in economic capital (a RAROC of 5%), it might be rejected in favor of a project that promises an $800,000 return but only needs $10 million in capital (a RAROC of 8%). The second project is more efficient at using the firm's precious capital.

Performance Evaluation: RAROC is used to judge the performance of managers and business units. A manager who delivers high profits by taking on massive, uncompensated risks will be exposed by a low RAROC. This encourages a culture of smart risk-taking, not just reckless pursuit of profit. It aligns the interests of the managers with the long-term health of the entire firm.

Pricing: For a bank, the price of a loan isn't just about the interest rate. The bank uses risk measures to calculate the economic capital needed to support that loan. The final price must be high enough to cover expected losses, operating costs, and provide an adequate return on that economic capital. If the calculated RAROC for a loan is below the hurdle rate, the bank might increase the interest rate or demand more collateral.

The choice of the underlying risk measure to calculate economic capital is crucial. The most common one is Value at Risk (VaR). VaR answers a simple but vital question: "What is the maximum amount of money I can expect to lose over a specific time period, at a specific confidence level?" For example, a 99% one-day VaR of $5 million means there is a 99% chance that the portfolio will not lose more than $5 million in the next day. That remaining 1% chance is what economic capital is there to cover. By aggregating the VaR from all business units, a firm can get a picture of its total risk and determine its total economic capital needs, which it can then allocate back to the units that created the risk in the first place.

Essentially, using risk measures in capital allocation transforms the process from a gut-feel, political tug-of-war into a disciplined, data-driven strategy. It ensures that capital, the lifeblood of any financial institution, flows to the areas where it can work most effectively, generating the best possible returns for an acceptable level of risk. It's the difference between navigating by the stars and navigating with a state-of-the-art GPS.

A Tour of the Financial World's Risk Toolkits

Different types of financial institutions are like different types of vehicles; they travel on different roads and face very different dangers. A race car (like an asset manager) is built for speed and worries about sharp turns, while an armored truck (like an insurer) is built for safety and worries about catastrophic attacks. Naturally, they use different dashboards and warning systems—or, in our world, different risk measures. Let's take a look at the specific tools used by the big players.

Banks: The Guardians of Liquidity and Credit

Banks are in a complex business. They take short-term deposits from people like you and me and turn them into long-term loans for businesses and homebuyers. Their biggest nightmares are twofold: credit risk (borrowers not paying back their loans) and market risk (the value of their investments plummeting). They also constantly worry about liquidity risk—what if too many depositors ask for their money back at once?

Value at Risk (VaR): This is the bread and butter of a bank's market risk management. A bank's trading desk holds a massive portfolio of stocks, bonds, currencies, and derivatives that fluctuate in value every second. VaR gives them a daily number that summarizes the potential loss. A senior manager can glance at the VaR figure and get an instant sense of the firm's market risk exposure. Regulators, like those enforcing the Basel Accords, also mandate that banks calculate VaR to determine how much capital they must hold against their trading activities.

Stress Testing and Scenario Analysis: While VaR is great for normal market conditions, it can fail during a crisis (the infamous 1% of the time). That's where stress testing comes in. Banks create doomsday scenarios—a stock market crash like 2008, a sudden spike in interest rates, a major sovereign default—and simulate how their portfolios would perform. This helps them understand their vulnerabilities and prepare for events that VaR might not capture. It's like a fire drill for their balance sheet.

Credit Risk Models: For their loan books, banks use sophisticated models (like CreditMetrics or KMV) to measure the probability of default (PD) for each borrower and the loss given default (LGD). By combining these, they can calculate the Expected Loss (EL), which is treated as a cost of doing business, and the Unexpected Loss (UL), which is what they need to hold economic capital against.

Asset Managers: Chasing Alpha
Asset managers are paid to grow their clients' money. Their world is all about performance and relative returns. They manage portfolios for mutual funds, high-net-worth individuals, and other institutions. Their primary focus is on market risk and how their performance stacks up against a benchmark (like the S&P 500 index).

Tracking Error: This is a crucial metric. It measures how much a portfolio's returns deviate from its benchmark. A low tracking error means the fund manager is closely following the index (like an index fund). A high tracking error suggests the manager is making active, aggressive bets to try and beat the benchmark. Clients need to know what they're paying for—a steady ride or a volatile one.

Sharpe Ratio: Developed by Nobel laureate William F. Sharpe, this is perhaps the most famous measure of risk-adjusted return. It's calculated as:

Sharpe Ratio= Standard Deviation of Portfolio
(Return of Portfolio−Risk-Free Rate)

In simple terms, it tells you how much excess return you're getting for each unit of volatility (risk) you take on. A higher Sharpe Ratio is better. It allows investors to compare different funds on a level playing field. A fund with a 20% return and high volatility might have a lower Sharpe Ratio than a fund with a 12% return and very low volatility.

Information Ratio: This is similar to the Sharpe Ratio but specifically for active managers. It measures the manager's ability to generate excess returns relative to a benchmark (this excess return is called "alpha") divided by the tracking error. It essentially answers: "How good is this manager at making bets that pay off, relative to the risk of those bets?"

Pension Funds: The Long Game

Pension funds have a unique challenge: they have very long-term liabilities. They need to make sure they have enough money to pay pensioners in 20, 30, or even 50 years. Their primary boogeyman is longevity risk (people living longer than expected) and asset-liability mismatch.

Asset-Liability Management (ALM): This isn't a single metric but a holistic framework. Pension funds map out their future liabilities (the pension payments they owe) and then construct an investment portfolio whose cash flows and risk profile match those liabilities as closely as possible. They are less concerned with short-term volatility and more concerned with ensuring they don't have a massive funding shortfall decades from now.

Surplus at Risk (SaR): This is a variation of VaR tailored for pension funds. Instead of just looking at the risk of the asset portfolio, it measures the risk to the fund's surplus (Assets - Liabilities). It answers the question: "What's the maximum amount our funding surplus could decrease over the next year with 95% confidence?" This directly links investment risk to the ultimate health of the pension plan.

Insurers: Bracing for Catastrophe

Insurers sell promises. They promise to pay for damages from a car accident, a house fire, or a hurricane. Their business is all about collecting premiums and hoping the claims that come in are less than what they've collected and earned on their investments. Their key risks are underwriting risk (mispricing policies or getting hit with more claims than expected) and catastrophe risk.

Probable Maximum Loss (PML): This is the cornerstone of property and casualty insurance. For an insurer covering homes in Florida, the PML is their estimate of the maximum loss they could suffer from a single, severe hurricane. They use complex catastrophe models (CAT models) that simulate thousands of potential weather events to arrive at this number. The entire business, from how much reinsurance they buy to how much capital they hold, is driven by the PML.

Stress Testing and Solvency Ratios: Like banks, insurers are heavily regulated and must prove they can withstand severe events. Regimes like Solvency II in Europe require insurers to conduct extensive stress tests. They must calculate their Solvency Capital Requirement (SCR), which is the amount of capital needed to survive a 1-in-200-year loss event. This ensures that even after a major disaster, the insurer will still be standing and able to pay its policyholders' claims. It's the ultimate financial strength test.

Backtesting and Simulation

Backtesting Investment Strategies: A Deep Dive
Backtesting is a critical process for any serious investor or trader. It's essentially a way to travel back in time to see how a specific investment strategy would have performed using historical data. This process allows you to test your ideas before risking any real capital. Think of it as a dress rehearsal for your money. By simulating trades based on past market conditions, you can gain valuable insights into a strategy's potential strengths and weaknesses. This guide will walk you through the core objectives of backtesting, the steps involved in the process, and how to make sense of the results.

1. The "Why": Objectives in Backtesting an Investment Strategy
Why do we backtest? The primary goal is to assess the viability of a trading or investment idea without putting actual money on the line. It's a foundational step in strategy development, moving an idea from a theoretical concept to a rigorously tested model. The objectives are multifaceted, aiming to build confidence and uncover potential flaws.

One of the most fundamental objectives is to determine profitability. At its core, an investment strategy is designed to make money. Backtesting provides a historical report card. Did the strategy generate positive returns over the period tested? Was the profit significant enough to justify the risks involved? This is the first and most obvious question that backtesting seeks to answer. It calculates key metrics like total profit or loss, giving you a baseline understanding of the strategy's historical performance. A strategy that fails to show profit in the past is unlikely to be a winner in the future, though past performance is never a guarantee.

Beyond simple profitability, a crucial objective is risk assessment. Every investment carries risk, and understanding the nature and magnitude of that risk is paramount. Backtesting helps quantify this. For example, it measures the "drawdown," which is the peak-to-trough decline during a specific period. A strategy might be profitable overall, but if it experiences terrifying 50% drawdowns, would you have the stomach to stick with it? Probably not. Backtesting exposes the bumpy ride you might have to endure. It also looks at volatility, often measured by standard deviation, to understand how wildly the returns might swing. By analyzing these risk metrics, you can decide if the strategy's risk profile aligns with your personal tolerance.

Another key objective is strategy validation and refinement. An idea might sound brilliant in your head, but the market has a way of humbling even the most confident investors. Backtesting is where theory meets reality. It validates whether the rules of your strategy—your entry signals, exit signals, and position sizing—actually work in a real-world data environment. Often, the initial backtest reveals weaknesses. Perhaps the exit signals are too slow, causing you to give back too much profit. Or maybe the entry signals are too frequent, leading to excessive trading costs. The backtest results provide the data needed to tweak and refine these rules. You can adjust parameters and run the test again, iterating until the strategy's performance improves and its logic is sound. This iterative process of testing and refining is central to developing a robust trading system.

Finally, a major objective is to check for robustness and overfitting. A strategy is robust if it performs well across different market conditions—bull markets, bear markets, and sideways markets. A backtest should cover a long period that includes various market environments to test this. Overfitting, on the other hand, is a major pitfall. It happens when a strategy is so finely tuned to the historical data that it looks perfect in the backtest but fails spectacularly in live trading. It's like creating a key that perfectly fits one specific old lock but can't open any other door. The objective here is to ensure the strategy isn't a "one-trick pony" that only worked during a specific, non-repeatable market phase. By testing on different timeframes and even different assets, you can gain confidence that your strategy has a genuine edge and isn't just a product of data mining.

2. The "How": Steps and Procedures in Backtesting
The process of backtesting can be broken down into a series of logical steps. While the tools and complexity can vary, the core procedure remains consistent. There are different ways to approach backtesting, primarily manual versus automated, each with its own procedures and trade-offs.

The first step, regardless of the method, is to define the strategy with absolute clarity. Your rules must be unambiguous. What specific conditions trigger a buy signal? What conditions trigger a sell signal? How much capital will be allocated to each trade? These rules must be so precise that a computer could execute them without any human discretion. For example, a rule might be: "Buy 100 shares of XYZ stock when its 50-day moving average crosses above its 200-day moving average. Sell when the 50-day moving average crosses back below the 200-day." Vague ideas like "buy when the stock looks strong" are not backtestable.

The second step is to gather high-quality historical data. This is a critical and often underestimated part of the process. The data must be accurate and cover a sufficiently long period to include different market regimes. For a stock trading strategy, you'll need daily (or intraday) price data (open, high, low, close) and volume. You must also account for corporate actions like stock splits, dividends, and mergers. A stock split, for instance, would dramatically alter the price, and without adjusting for it, your backtest results would be nonsensical. Garbage in, garbage out. Poor data will inevitably lead to flawed and misleading results.

Once you have your rules and data, the third step is the simulation itself. This is where manual and automated backtesting diverge.

Manual backtesting is the simpler, more intuitive approach. Here, you literally scroll back through historical charts, one candle at a time, and simulate your trades. You would have a spreadsheet or a journal to record your hypothetical trades based on your rules. When your entry signal appears, you note the entry price. You then advance the chart until an exit signal appears, and you record the exit price and calculate the profit or loss. This procedure is slow and labor-intensive, but it has a key advantage: it helps you develop a deep, intuitive feel for how your strategy behaves in different market conditions. You see the wins and losses play out visually, which can be a powerful learning experience.

Automated backtesting, in contrast, uses software to do the heavy lifting. You code your strategy's rules into a backtesting platform (like TradingView, MetaTrader, or custom scripts in Python). The software then crunches through years of historical data in seconds, executing your rules and generating a detailed performance report. This procedure is far more efficient and allows for rapid testing of many different ideas and parameter variations. It removes human emotion and error from the simulation process, ensuring the rules are followed perfectly every time. The challenge here lies in needing some programming knowledge or familiarity with the specific platform's language.

The final step is analyzing the results, which we'll cover in the next section. However, an important procedure to contrast here is the concept of in-sample vs. out-of-sample testing. When you develop and refine your strategy, you are using a specific chunk of historical data—this is your "in-sample" data. The danger of overfitting arises here. To combat this, you should reserve a separate portion of data that you don't look at during the development phase. This is your "out-of-sample" data. After you have finalized your strategy based on the in-sample results, you run one final test on the out-of-sample data. If the strategy performs similarly well on this unseen data, it provides much stronger evidence that the strategy is robust and not overfitted. This procedure is a cornerstone of professional quantitative analysis.

3. The "What": Interpreting Metrics and Visuals
After the simulation is complete, you are presented with a report filled with numbers and charts. Understanding what these metrics and visuals mean is essential for making an informed decision about the strategy's future. It's not just about looking at the final profit; it's about understanding the journey the strategy took to get there.

Let's start with the core performance metrics. Total Net Profit is the most obvious one—it's the bottom line. But it should be looked at in conjunction with the Profit Factor, which is the gross profit divided by the gross loss. A profit factor above 2.0 is often considered very good, meaning the strategy made twice as much money on its winning trades as it lost on its losing trades. Another key metric is the Win Rate (or percentage of profitable trades). A high win rate might feel good, but it's not the whole story. A strategy could win 90% of the time but have one catastrophic loss that wipes out all the small wins. This is why you must also look at the Average Win and Average Loss. A healthy strategy typically has an average win that is significantly larger than its average loss.

Next are the risk metrics, which are arguably more important. The Maximum Drawdown is paramount. It tells you the largest percentage drop your account would have suffered. This figure represents the potential pain you would have had to endure. If you can't stomach that kind of drop, the strategy isn't right for you, no matter how profitable it is. Another metric is the Sharpe Ratio, which measures risk-adjusted return. It tells you how much return you are getting for each unit of risk (volatility) you take on. A higher Sharpe Ratio (typically above 1.0) is better, as it indicates a more efficient strategy.

Visuals often tell the story better than numbers alone. The most important visual is the equity curve. This is a graph that plots the growth of your hypothetical account balance over time. An ideal equity curve should be a relatively smooth line moving from the bottom-left to the top-right. A jagged, volatile equity curve, even if it ends up higher, indicates a risky and stressful strategy. If the curve goes flat for long periods, it means the strategy can stagnate. If it suddenly nosedives, it reveals a vulnerability to certain market conditions.

Another useful visual is a drawdown plot. This chart shows the periods when the account was below its previous peak. It helps you visualize the length and depth of the losing streaks. Seeing a visual representation of a 20-month period where the strategy went nowhere but down is much more impactful than just reading a "Max Drawdown" number.

Finally, some backtesting reports provide a trade distribution plot or a monthly/yearly returns breakdown. These visuals can help you spot patterns. Does the strategy only perform well in certain months? Does it struggle during periods of high volatility? This deeper analysis helps you understand the character of your strategy and the environments in which it is most likely to thrive or fail. By combining these metrics and visuals, you can build a complete picture of your investment strategy's historical behavior, allowing you to move forward with a much greater degree of confidence.

Spotting the Ghosts in the Machine: Problems in a Backtest

Think of backtesting an investment strategy as watching a recording of a past sports game where you already know the final score. It's incredibly easy to look back and say, "I knew they should have passed the ball there!" because you're armed with the knowledge of the outcome. In the world of investing, this is the fundamental challenge of backtesting. You're trying to see how a strategy would have performed in the past, but it's dangerously easy to let knowledge of the future—even accidentally—seep into your test and create a picture that looks far rosier than reality. Identifying these problems is less about complex math and more about being a good detective, looking for clues that your beautiful, profitable strategy is just an illusion.

One of the most common and sneaky culprits is look-ahead bias. This is the cardinal sin of backtesting. It happens when your simulation uses information that wouldn't have been available at the moment of the decision. Imagine your strategy is to buy a stock if its closing price is 5% higher than its opening price. In a sloppy backtest, the computer might look at the end-of-day data, see that the stock met the criteria, and simulate a purchase at the opening price of that day. It's a paradox; the decision to buy at the open was made using information from the close. You essentially built a time machine into your code. A real-world trader standing at the market open has no clue what the closing price will be. This single flaw can turn a mediocre strategy into a world-beating one on paper. It requires painstaking attention to detail, ensuring your data timestamps are perfect and that every decision is based only on what was known at that precise moment.

Then there's the equally deceptive problem of survivorship bias. Picture this: you want to study the common habits of successful coffee shops. So, you walk down the main street and interview the owners of all the thriving cafes that are open today. You might conclude that all successful cafes have minimalist decor and serve avocado toast. But what you've missed are the dozens of cafes that went out of business over the past ten years—the ones with dated decor, the ones that failed for countless other reasons. You've only studied the survivors. In investing, this happens when you run a backtest on a stock index, like the S&P 500, as it exists today. Your test automatically filters out all the companies that went bankrupt, got acquired, or were delisted over the years. Your strategy looks brilliant because it was only tested on the winners. A proper backtest needs to use a point-in-time database that includes all the "dead" stocks, ensuring your strategy is forced to navigate the same corporate graveyard that real investors face.

Another major issue is data snooping, or as it's more formally known, overfitting. This is what happens when you torture the data until it confesses. You might test hundreds or thousands of different rules and parameters. "Maybe I should buy when the 47-day moving average crosses the

182-day moving average, but only on a Tuesday if the market is up more than 0.3%." Eventually, you'll stumble upon a set of rules that perfectly fits the historical data's random noise. You haven't discovered a timeless market principle; you've just written a perfect description of the past. This "perfect" strategy will almost certainly fall apart when it encounters a future that doesn't look exactly like the period you tested it on. It's like creating a key that perfectly fits one very specific, old lock. The moment you try it on a new lock, it's useless. To avoid this, you should have a clear hypothesis before you start testing and use out-of-sample data (a chunk of history you kept hidden during the development phase) to validate your findings.

Finally, even a technically perfect backtest can be a fantasy if it ignores real-world frictions. Your simulation might show a strategy making thousands of trades and generating a 30% annual return. But it often forgets the little things that eat away at profits. Transaction costs, like brokerage commissions and fees, act like a small tax on every single trade. Slippage is another killer; it's the difference between the price you expected to trade at and the price you actually got. In a fast-moving market, by the time your order is executed, the price may have moved against you. And of course, there are taxes on your gains. These seemingly small details can accumulate and turn a profitable strategy into a losing one. A realistic backtest must rigorously account for these costs, providing a net return that reflects what you might actually have taken home.

Learning from Ghosts: Evaluating a Historical Scenario Analysis

While backtesting tries to simulate a strategy running continuously through history, a historical scenario analysis is different. It's a focused financial "fire drill." You pick a specific, terrifying period from the past—like the 2008

Global Financial Crisis, the 2000 Dot-Com Bubble burst, or the sharp COVID-19 crash of 2020—and you transport your current portfolio back in time to see how it would have fared. The goal isn't to see if your strategy "works," but to understand your portfolio's breaking points and to prepare yourself psychologically for severe market stress. Evaluating and interpreting this analysis is an art, blending quantitative results with qualitative judgment.

The first step in evaluation is to question the relevance of the chosen scenario. History doesn't repeat itself, but it often rhymes. You need to ask yourself: how much does that past event "rhyme" with the risks we face today? For example, testing a portfolio of high-growth tech stocks against the dot-com bubble of 2000 is incredibly relevant because the underlying theme—speculative fervor in technology—is a recurring one. However, testing that same portfolio against the 1970s oil crisis might be less insightful, as the economic drivers of that crisis (geopolitical oil shocks, stagflation) are fundamentally different from the risks inherent in today's tech sector. A good evaluation involves a thoughtful justification for why a particular historical event is a plausible stress test for your specific collection of assets today. You must also consider the severity and duration of the event. The 2008 crisis was a deep, prolonged collapse that tested investor endurance, while the 2020 crash was a sudden, violent plunge that tested liquidity and nerve. Both are valuable, but they test different things.

Once the analysis is run, interpreting the results goes far beyond a single headline number. Let's say the report shows your portfolio would have lost 35% during the 2008 scenario. The real value is in the details. The first thing to interpret is contribution to loss. Which of your assets were the biggest culprits? Did your stocks all fall together, or did certain sectors get hit harder? More importantly, did your so-called "safe" assets, like bonds, do their job of cushioning the blow? If your bonds also lost significant value, it might reveal a flaw in your diversification strategy. The analysis should allow you to see the weak links in your portfolio's armor.

Next, you must interpret the key performance metrics in human terms. The most important of these is the maximum drawdown. This isn't just an abstract percentage; it's the single largest peak-to-trough drop your portfolio would have experienced. A 35% drawdown means that for every $100,000 you had invested at the peak, it would have shrunk to $65,000 at the bottom. The critical interpretation here is a gut check: could you have stomach that? Would you have panicked and sold at the worst possible moment? Another vital piece of the story is the time to recovery. How many months or years would it have taken for your portfolio to climb back to its previous high? A drawdown is painful, but a drawdown that takes a decade to recover from can derail major life goals, like retirement. Interpreting this metric is about understanding the potential opportunity cost and the long-term impact of a severe market shock.

Finally, a crucial part of the evaluation is to humbly acknowledge the limitations of the exercise. The biggest caveat is that the next crisis will never be an exact replica of the last one. Using the 2008 crisis as a model might prepare you for a banking collapse, but it might not prepare you for a global pandemic or a new type of technological disruption. Furthermore, the analysis relies on a huge assumption: that your current assets will behave exactly as their historical counterparts did. For new asset classes like cryptocurrencies or complex derivatives that didn't exist in 2008, analysts must use proxies, which are essentially educated guesses. Therefore, the results should be viewed not as a precise prediction, but as a well-informed, plausible story about what could happen. It's a tool for building resilience and managing expectations, not a crystal ball.

Monte Carlo vs. Historical Simulation: Peering into the Future

Imagine you're trying to predict the financial weather for your investment portfolio over the next month. You want to understand the possible storms and sunny days that might lie ahead. Two popular forecasting tools at your disposal are Historical Simulation and Monte Carlo Simulation. While both aim to map out future possibilities, they do so in fundamentally different, almost philosophically opposite, ways.

The Historical Simulation: Driving by Looking in the Rear-View Mirror

The historical simulation method is the more straightforward of the two. It operates on a simple, powerful, and somewhat stubborn assumption: the future will be a replay of the past.

Think of it like this. To predict tomorrow's market movements, this method grabs a big chunk of actual, historical data—say, the daily price changes of all the stocks in your portfolio over the last two years (about 500 trading days). It then treats each of those past days as a possible scenario for tomorrow.

Scenario 1: What would happen to my portfolio if the market behaved exactly like it did on January 5th, two years ago? You apply those specific price changes to your current portfolio and calculate the profit or loss.

Scenario 2: What if tomorrow is a repeat of January 6th? You do the same calculation.

...Scenario 500: And what about the last day in your data set?

After running your current portfolio through every single one of these 500 historical "days," you'll have a list of 500 possible outcomes for tomorrow. By arranging these outcomes from worst to best, you can get a rich picture of your risk. You can pinpoint the value at the 5th percentile and say, "There is a 5% chance my portfolio will lose this amount or more," which is a concept known as Value at Risk (VaR).

The beauty of this approach is its simplicity and lack of assumptions. You don't need to guess the statistical distribution of returns (e.g., are they a perfect bell curve?). You don't need to estimate how different stocks move together (their correlation). The data speaks for itself, capturing the real-world weirdness, fat tails (extreme events), and complex relationships that actually occurred.

However, its greatest strength is also its most profound weakness. The historical method is fundamentally backward-looking. It is completely blind to any event or combination of events that hasn't happened in its lookback window. If your historical data is from a period of calm, low volatility, the simulation will predict nothing but smooth sailing ahead, leaving you utterly unprepared for a sudden squall. It's like preparing for a blizzard in Miami just because it snowed there once in 1977; the past isn't always a reliable map for the future.

The Monte Carlo Simulation: Building the Future from Scratch

If historical simulation is like re-watching old game tapes, Monte Carlo simulation is like creating a sophisticated video game engine that can generate entirely new, never-before-seen levels. It doesn't replay the past; it simulates new futures based on a set of rules and assumptions.

This approach requires more upfront work. First, you must become an architect of your financial world. You need to make educated guesses about the key drivers of your portfolio's value. For each stock, you'll need to specify its expected return and its volatility (how much its price tends to bounce around). Crucially, you also need to define how these stocks move in relation to one another—their correlation. Does Stock A tend to go up when Stock B goes down?

You formalize these assumptions into a mathematical model, often assuming that stock returns follow a particular statistical pattern, like the well-known normal distribution (the "bell curve").

Once your model is built, the Monte Carlo engine kicks in. It uses a random number generator to create thousands, or even hundreds of thousands, of hypothetical "tomorrows."

Trial 1: The engine generates a random number for each stock, consistent with its assumed volatility and its correlation with other stocks, to simulate one possible set of price changes for tomorrow. It calculates the portfolio's resulting profit or loss.

Trial 2: It does it all over again, generating a new set of random numbers and a completely new outcome.

...Trial 10,000: It repeats this process over and over.

The result is a vast, artificially generated data set of potential futures. Like the historical method, you can sort these outcomes to calculate VaR or other risk metrics.

The huge advantage of Monte Carlo is its flexibility and forward-looking nature. You are not constrained by what has happened before. You can model extreme events that are theoretically possible but haven't yet occurred. You can also easily stress-test your assumptions by asking, "What if volatility suddenly doubles, or the correlation between stocks and bonds breaks down?"

The catch, however, is that the simulation is only as good as its underlying assumptions. This is the "garbage in, garbage out" problem. If you incorrectly specify the distributions or correlations, your shiny, complex model could produce results that are precisely calculated but dangerously wrong. It requires more statistical expertise and is computationally more intensive, but it offers a far more dynamic and customizable lens through which to view the landscape of future risk.

The Art and Science of Simulation: Inputs, Decisions, and Interpretation

Running a simulation is like conducting a grand experiment in a digital laboratory. You're building a model of a real-world situation—like launching a new product, planning a factory expansion, or managing a retirement fund—and then letting it run through thousands of possible futures to see what might happen. Successfully navigating this process boils down to three key stages: choosing your inputs, defining your decisions, and, most importantly, interpreting the results.

The Ingredients: Choosing Your Inputs

The inputs are the raw materials of your simulation. They are the uncertain variables, the things you don't know for sure but that will ultimately determine your success or failure. The quality of your simulation rests entirely on how well you define these inputs.

Imagine you're modeling the potential profit from opening a new coffee shop. What are your key uncertainties?

Market Size: How many people will walk past your shop each day? You don't know the exact number, but you can estimate a range.

Conversion Rate: What percentage of those people will actually come in and buy something?

Average Spend: How much will the average customer spend? Will they just get a small coffee or a latte and a pastry?

Variable Costs: How much will the coffee beans and milk for each cup cost? This price might fluctuate.

For each input, you must not only estimate a range of possible values but also choose a probability distribution that best describes its behavior. This is a critical step.

A Uniform Distribution is used when any value within a range is equally likely. For example, a competitor's reaction time might be anywhere from one to six months.

A Normal Distribution (the bell curve) is perfect for things that have a clear average, with values becoming less likely the further they are from that average, like the daily amount of milk used.

A Triangular Distribution is a practical choice when you can confidently estimate a minimum, a maximum, and a "most likely" value, but don't have enough data for a more complex distribution. This could be used for the initial marketing cost.

Choosing the right inputs and their distributions is where deep business knowledge meets statistical science. A poorly chosen input can poison the entire simulation.

The Levers: Making Decisions

While inputs are the elements of uncertainty you can't control, decisions are the levers you can pull. These are the strategic choices you are trying to test. In our coffee shop model, the key decision might be the price of a cup of coffee. Should you price it at $3.00, $4.00, or $5.00?

The simulation's purpose is to see how your decision plays out against the backdrop of thousands of random scenarios generated by the inputs. You can run the entire simulation three times: once for each price point. By doing so, you're not just asking, "What will my profit be?" You're asking a much more powerful question: "Which pricing strategy gives me the best chance of success, considering all the things I can't control?" The decision is the variable you are actively testing to find the optimal path forward.

The Story: Interpreting the Simulation Output

A simulation doesn't give you a single, magical number as an answer. If it did, it wouldn't be very useful. Instead, it gives you a distribution of possible outcomes. The final step is to interpret this rich tapestry of data to make an informed decision.

When you run the coffee shop simulation for a $4.00 price point, you might get 10,000 different possible annual profit figures. The most common way to visualize this is with a histogram, which is a bar chart showing how frequently different profit levels occurred in the simulation.

From this output, you can extract crucial insights:

Expected Outcome: The average profit across all 10,000 trials. This is your most likely result, but it's only part of the story.

Measure of Risk: The standard deviation of the outcomes tells you how spread out the results are. A wide distribution means a very risky venture; a narrow one implies more certainty.

Probabilistic Statements: This is the real power. You can now answer questions that a simple spreadsheet can't.

"What is the probability that we will lose money?" (i.e., the percentage of trials where profit was less than zero).

"What is the probability of achieving our target profit of $50,000?"

"What is the range of profit we can expect with 90% confidence?"

By comparing the output distributions for your different pricing decisions ($3, $4, and $5), you can make a holistic choice. Maybe the $5 price point has the highest average profit, but it also comes with a scary 30% chance of losing money. The $4 price point might have a slightly lower average profit but only a 5% chance of loss. The simulation gives you a clear view of the risk-reward trade-off, empowering you to choose a path that aligns with your risk appetite.

Sensitivity Analysis: Finding Your Model's Pressure Points
After building a complex financial model or simulation, you're often left with a single-number output, like a project's Net Present Value (NPV) or a company's projected earnings per share. But this single number is built on a foundation of dozens of assumptions. Sensitivity analysis is the process of systematically poking and prodding that foundation to see which assumptions are holding up the most weight. It answers a simple, vital question: "Which inputs, if I get them wrong, will have the biggest impact on my final answer?"

How It Works: Isolating One Variable at a Time
Imagine you're a real estate developer analyzing a proposal to build a new apartment complex. Your model calculates the project's NPV, and your base case shows a healthy positive value. But this NPV depends on several key assumptions you've made:

Construction Costs per Square Foot: Your best guess is $150.

Average Monthly Rent: You project $2,000 per unit.

Occupancy Rate: You assume it will average 95%.

Exit Capitalization Rate: The rate you use to estimate the building's sale price in 10 years, which you assume is 5%.

A simulation would vary all of these at once to see the range of possible NPVs. Sensitivity analysis takes a more disciplined, one-at-a-time approach.

The Process:

Establish the Base Case: Calculate the NPV using all your initial "best guess" assumptions. Let's say it's $2.5 million.

Flex One Variable: Start with construction costs. You ask, "What happens to the NPV if costs are 10% higher ($165) or 10% lower ($135) than my base case?" You re-calculate the NPV for both scenarios, keeping all other variables (rent, occupancy, etc.) fixed at their base case values.

Record the Impact: You note how much the NPV changed. Perhaps the higher costs dropped the NPV to $1.8 million, and the lower costs raised it to $3.2 million.

Reset and Repeat: You reset the construction cost back to the base case of $150. Now, you move to the next variable: average rent. You test what happens if rent is 10% higher or lower, again keeping everything else constant. You continue this methodical process for every key input in your model.

The Grand Reveal: The Tornado Chart
The real power of sensitivity analysis comes from how you present the results. The most effective tool for this is a Tornado Chart.

A Tornado Chart is a special type of bar chart that stacks the results for each variable, with the longest bar at the top and the shortest at the bottom, resembling a tornado on its side. Each horizontal bar shows the range of outcomes for your output (NPV in our case) when that specific input is changed.

In our real estate example, the chart might look like this:

The top bar, labeled "Exit Capitalization Rate," might be the widest. This tells you that even a small change in the final sale price assumption has a massive impact on the project's profitability. A lower cap rate (higher price) sends the NPV soaring, while a higher cap rate (lower price) could sink the entire project.

The next bar might be "Average Monthly Rent," showing it has a significant but smaller impact.

Further down, the "Construction Costs" bar might be even narrower.

At the very bottom might be something like "Annual Maintenance Costs," which has a barely noticeable effect on the NPV.

Interpreting the Tornado Chart is incredibly intuitive. It instantly directs your attention to what matters most. The variables at the top are your project's critical pressure points. These are the assumptions that inject the most uncertainty and risk into your forecast.

This insight is pure gold. It tells you where to focus your resources. If the exit cap rate is the most sensitive variable, you should spend more time researching the future real estate market, consulting with brokers, and analyzing comparable sales data to narrow the uncertainty around that number. You might also structure the deal to mitigate this risk, perhaps by negotiating a guaranteed sale price. For the variables at the bottom of the chart, you can be more relaxed; your initial "best guess" is likely good enough, as even a large error won't derail the outcome.

In essence, sensitivity analysis acts as a powerful diagnostic tool. It deconstructs your model's complexity and gives you a clear, rank-ordered list of what you should be worrying about the most. It transforms a sea of assumptions into a focused action plan for managing risk.

Subject 2: Ethical and Professional Standards

Code of Ethics and Standards of Professional Conduct

Understanding the CFA Institute's Ethical Framework
The CFA (Chartered Financial Analyst) designation is one of the most respected credentials in the investment management profession. At its very core lies a profound commitment to ethics. This isn't just about rules; it's about building a foundation of trust in the global financial markets. For CFA Institute members and candidates aspiring to earn the charter, adhering to a strict ethical framework isn't optional—it's mandatory. This framework is built upon two key pillars: the Code of Ethics, which provides the overarching principles, and the Standards of Professional Conduct, which offer specific, actionable rules. Let's explore these components to understand the profound ethical responsibilities they entail.

Part 1: The Six Components of the Code of Ethics
The Code of Ethics acts as the moral compass for investment professionals. It's a set of six core principles that every CFA member and candidate must pledge to uphold. These principles are broad, serving as the foundation upon which the more detailed Standards are built. They are promises made to clients, employers, the public, and the profession itself.

1. Act with Integrity, Competence, Diligence, and Respect

This first component is arguably the most encompassing. It demands that professionals act with unwavering honesty and integrity in all their dealings. It's about being truthful and not misleading others. Competence means you must have the necessary knowledge and skills to do your job effectively; if you don't, you must take steps to acquire them or refrain from the task. Diligence is about being thorough, careful, and prompt in your work. You can't be lazy or sloppy. Finally, acting with respect means treating everyone—clients, colleagues, competitors—in a professional and courteous manner. It's about fostering a culture of mutual respect that elevates the entire industry. This principle is the bedrock of professionalism, ensuring that trust is never compromised.

2. Place the Integrity of the Investment Profession and the Interests of Clients Above Personal Interests

This is the fiduciary principle at its heart. It requires investment professionals to be selfless. Your clients' financial well-being must always come before your own desire for personal gain. This means avoiding situations where your interests conflict with your clients' interests. For example, you shouldn't recommend an investment just because it pays you a higher commission. Similarly, you have a duty to uphold the integrity of the entire profession. This means you should not engage in any conduct that would damage the reputation or trustworthiness of the capital markets. The markets function on trust, and this principle is designed to protect that trust above all else.

3. Use Reasonable Care and Exercise Independent Professional Judgment

This component focuses on the quality of your work. "Reasonable care" means you must act as a prudent and competent professional would in the same situation. It involves a thoughtful and deliberate process in your analysis and recommendations. You can't just follow the herd or make decisions on a whim. The second part, "independent professional judgment," is equally crucial. Your advice should be objective and untainted by outside influences. You shouldn't let your boss, a client, or anyone else pressure you into making a recommendation that you don't genuinely believe is in the client's best interest. Your analysis and your voice must be your own, based on rigorous and unbiased work.

4. Practice and Encourage Others to Practice in a Professional and Ethical Manner

Ethics is not a solitary pursuit. This principle extends your responsibility beyond your own actions to the actions of those around you. You have an obligation to not only act ethically yourself but also to encourage your peers, colleagues, and the industry at large to do the same. If you see unethical behavior, you have a responsibility to take action—which might mean reporting it or simply promoting a culture where such behavior is not tolerated. This creates a ripple effect, where one person's commitment to ethics can influence many others, thereby strengthening the entire profession from within.

5. Promote the Integrity and Viability of the Global Capital Markets

This component elevates the professional's duty from the individual client to the system as a whole. The global capital markets are the engine of economic growth, and their health depends on fairness and transparency. Professionals have a duty to act in a way that fosters market integrity. This means not engaging in market manipulation, insider trading, or any activity that would give some participants an unfair advantage. It's about being a good steward of the markets, ensuring they are a level playing field where capital can be allocated efficiently and investors can have confidence in the system.

6. Maintain and Improve Professional Competence

The financial world is constantly evolving. New products, strategies, and regulations emerge all the time. This final component of the Code dictates that you can't rest on your laurels. It establishes a commitment to lifelong learning. You must actively work to maintain and improve your skills and knowledge throughout your career. This can be done through continuing education, reading professional journals, attending seminars, or pursuing further credentials. It ensures that the advice you provide to clients is not just ethical but also current, relevant, and informed by the latest industry practices.

Part 2: The Seven Standards of Professional Conduct
If the Code of Ethics is the constitution, the Standards of Professional Conduct are the laws. They provide detailed, specific rules that elaborate on the principles in the Code. There are seven Standards, each covering a different area of professional practice.

I. Professionalism

This first standard is broad and covers the core tenets of being a professional. It's broken down into four sub-sections:

Knowledge of the Law: You must understand and comply with all applicable laws, rules, and regulations of any country or regulatory body governing your activities. If there's a conflict, you must follow the stricter law or rule. You cannot plead ignorance as an excuse for a violation.

Independence and Objectivity: You must use reasonable care and judgment to achieve and maintain independence and objectivity in your professional activities. You must not offer, solicit, or accept any gift or compensation that could be reasonably expected to compromise your own or another's independence.

Misrepresentation: You cannot knowingly make any misrepresentations related to investment analysis, recommendations, or other professional activities. This means you can't lie, plagiarize, or present someone else's work as your own.

Misconduct: You must not engage in any professional conduct involving dishonesty, fraud, or deceit or commit any act that reflects adversely on your professional reputation, integrity, or competence.

II. Integrity of Capital Markets

This standard focuses on protecting the fairness and efficiency of the markets.

Material Nonpublic Information: If you possess information that is both "material" (meaning it would likely affect a security's price) and "nonpublic," you cannot act on it or cause others to act on it. This is the cornerstone of insider trading prevention.

Market Manipulation: You must not engage in practices that distort prices or artificially inflate trading volume with the intent to mislead market participants. This prohibits spreading false rumors or engaging in manipulative trading schemes.

III. Duties to Clients

This is a critical standard that outlines your responsibilities to the people you serve.

Loyalty, Prudence, and Care: This is the fiduciary duty. You have a duty of loyalty to your clients and must act with reasonable care and exercise prudent judgment. You must always act for the benefit of your clients and place their interests before your employer's or your own interests.

Fair Dealing: You must deal fairly and objectively with all clients when providing investment analysis, making recommendations, or taking investment action. You cannot favor some clients over others. For example, if a hot new stock is recommended, it must be offered to all suitable clients, not just a select few.

Suitability: When you are in an advisory relationship with a client, you must make a reasonable inquiry into their investment experience, risk tolerance, and financial situation. Your recommendations must be suitable for their specific circumstances.

Performance Presentation: When communicating investment performance information, you must make reasonable efforts to ensure that it is fair, accurate, and complete. You can't cherry-pick results to make performance look better than it was.

Preservation of Confidentiality: You must keep information about current, former, and prospective clients confidential unless the client permits disclosure, the information concerns illegal activities, or you are legally required to disclose it.

IV. Duties to Employers

Your ethical duties extend to the firm that employs you.

Loyalty: In matters related to your employment, you must act for the benefit of your employer and not deprive them of your skills, divulge confidential information, or otherwise cause harm to your employer. However, this duty does not require you to subordinate your clients' interests.

Additional Compensation Arrangements: You must not accept gifts, benefits, or compensation that competes with or might create a conflict of interest with your employer's interest unless you get written consent from all parties involved.

Responsibilities of Supervisors: If you are in a supervisory role, you must make reasonable efforts to ensure that anyone subject to your supervision complies with applicable laws, rules, regulations, and the Code and Standards.

V. Investment Analysis, Recommendations, and Actions

This standard governs the work you do as an analyst or portfolio manager.

Diligence and Reasonable Basis: Your investment analysis and recommendations must have a reasonable and adequate basis, supported by appropriate research and investigation. You must be able to back up your conclusions.

Communication with Clients and Prospective Clients: You must disclose the basic format and general principles of the investment processes you use. You must disclose significant limitations and risks. You must distinguish between fact and opinion in your reports.

Record Retention: You must develop and maintain appropriate records to support your investment analysis, recommendations, and other investment-related communications with clients.

VI. Conflicts of Interest

Conflicts are common in the industry; the key is to manage them properly.

Disclosure of Conflicts: You must make full and fair disclosure of all matters that could reasonably be expected to impair your independence and objectivity or interfere with your duties to clients or your employer. This must be done prominently and in plain language.

Priority of Transactions: Investment transactions for clients and employers must have priority over transactions in which you are the beneficial owner. This means you can't buy or sell a stock for your own account ahead of a client trade.

Referral Fees: You must disclose to your employer, clients, and prospective clients, as appropriate, any compensation or benefit received for the recommendation of products or services.

VII. Responsibilities as a CFA Institute Member or CFA Candidate

Finally, this standard covers your conduct related to the CFA program itself.

Conduct as Participants in CFA Institute Programs: You must not engage in any conduct that compromises the reputation or integrity of the CFA Institute or the CFA designation or the integrity, validity, or security of the CFA exams.

Reference to CFA Institute, the CFA Designation, and the CFA Program: When referring to your membership, designation, or candidacy, you must not misrepresent or exaggerate the meaning or implications of it. You can't, for instance, promise "superior" investment returns just because you are a charterholder.

By internalizing and applying this comprehensive ethical framework, CFA members and candidates not only protect their clients and employers but also contribute to a more trustworthy and transparent global financial system for everyone.

Guidance for Standards I-VII

A Practical Guide to the CFA Code of Ethics and Standards

The CFA Institute's Code of Ethics and Standards of Professional Conduct are the bedrock of the investment management profession. They aren't just a set of rules to memorize for an exam; they represent a fundamental commitment to fairness, integrity, and putting clients first. Understanding these principles is one thing, but truly mastering them means knowing how they apply in the real world—the messy, complex world of finance where gray areas are common. This guide aims to bring these standards to life through practical examples and offer clear, actionable steps to build a professional environment that champions ethical behavior.

Applying the Code and Standards to Real-World Situations

Demonstrating a thorough knowledge of the CFA Code and Standards goes beyond simple recitation. It requires the ability to see a situation, identify the potential ethical conflicts, and apply the correct principles to find a solution. Let's explore some common scenarios.

Scenario 1: The "Hot Tip"

Imagine you are a portfolio manager, and during a casual lunch, a friend who works as an executive at a publicly traded tech company mentions that their upcoming quarterly earnings will significantly beat analyst expectations. This is clearly material, nonpublic information. Acting on this would be a direct violation of Standard II(A) - Material Nonpublic Information.

Wrong Action: You immediately buy shares of the company for your personal account and for your clients' portfolios to capitalize on the expected price jump.

Correct Application: The standard is unequivocal. You must not act on this information or cause others to act on it. The most prudent course of action is to do nothing with the information in terms of trading. You should also make reasonable efforts to encourage your friend to publicly disclose the information. If you have supervisory responsibilities, you should also document the situation and inform your compliance department. This protects you, your clients, and the integrity of the market. You are safeguarding the principle that all market participants should have access to the same information.

Scenario 2: The Lavish "Educational" Trip

A brokerage firm that executes a significant volume of trades for your clients offers you an all-expenses-paid trip to a luxury resort for a "due diligence" conference. While there are some presentations, the agenda is mostly filled with golf, fine dining, and entertainment. This situation falls under Standard I(B) - Independence and Objectivity.

Wrong Action: Accepting the trip without question. Such an extravagant gift could compromise your independence and objectivity. In the future, you might feel obligated to direct more trades to that brokerage firm, even if they aren't offering the best execution for your clients. This isn't about their service; it's about the gift influencing your professional judgment.

Correct Application: You must evaluate whether the offer is reasonable and could be perceived as impairing your judgment. A modest lunch is one thing; a luxury vacation is another. The best practice is to decline the offer. If your firm has a policy, it might allow for attendance but require that your firm pays for all travel, accommodation, and entertainment expenses. This removes the conflict of interest. The goal is to ensure that your decisions are based solely on what is best for your clients, not on who gives you the best perks. This upholds the trust your clients place in you to act as their fiduciary.

Scenario 3: The Social Media Dilemma

You're proud of a stock you recommended that has performed exceptionally well. You post on a personal social media account, "So glad I got my clients into XYZ Corp. It's up 50% since my 'buy' rating! #winning #stockmarket." This seemingly harmless post could violate several standards, including Standard III(B) - Fair Dealing and Standard I(C) - Misrepresentation.

Wrong Action: The post is problematic because it highlights a winning pick without providing the full context. Are you showing all your recommendations, including the ones that didn't do well? This is a form of misrepresentation by omission. Furthermore, if you shared this "buy" rating with some clients before others, it could be a violation of fair dealing.

Correct Application: Communication with clients and the public must be professional and balanced. All performance presentations should be fair, accurate, and complete. If you are going to discuss performance, it should be done through official firm channels and in a way that presents a balanced picture over a relevant time period, not just cherry-picking winners. Social media is a powerful tool, but it must be used with extreme care, ensuring that all communications adhere to the same rigorous standards as a formal client report.

Practices and Procedures to Prevent Violations
A strong ethical culture doesn't happen by accident. It's built through deliberate, consistent, and well-designed practices and procedures. For both individuals and firms, preventing violations is far more effective than dealing with them after the fact. Here are key recommendations.

1. Create a Culture of Integrity from the Top Down

The single most important factor in preventing ethical breaches is a clear commitment from senior leadership.

Adoption of the Code: Firms should formally adopt the CFA Code and Standards as their own internal policy. This isn't just a poster on the wall; it should be integrated into employee handbooks, training manuals, and annual attestations.

Lead by Example: Senior managers must embody the principles they espouse. If junior analysts see supervisors cutting ethical corners, they will assume that behavior is acceptable. Leadership must be vocal and visible in their support for ethical conduct.

2. Develop Robust and Clear Policies

Written policies eliminate ambiguity and provide clear guidance for employees.

Personal Trading Policies: Every firm needs a strict, clear policy on personal trading. This should include pre-clearance requirements for trades, mandated holding periods to discourage short-term speculation, and a list of restricted securities (e.g., companies the firm is actively researching). This directly addresses conflicts of interest (Standard VI(B) - Priority of Transactions).

Gifts and Entertainment Policy: Establish clear, quantitative limits on the value of gifts that can be accepted. For instance, any gift over $100 must be pre-approved by the compliance department. This provides a black-and-white rule that helps employees navigate situations involving Standard I(B) - Independence and Objectivity.

Information Barriers (Firewalls): For firms with multiple departments (e.g., investment banking and asset management), it's crucial to have information firewalls. This means physically separating departments, restricting access to electronic files, and implementing procedures to prevent the flow of material nonpublic information between them. This is a structural defense against violations of Standard II(A).

3. Implement Ongoing Education and Training

Ethics are not a "one-and-done" topic. Continuous education keeps the principles top-of-mind.

New Hire Orientation: Every new employee, regardless of their role, should receive comprehensive training on the Code and Standards and the firm's specific policies.

Annual Ethics Refresher: At least once a year, all employees should participate in mandatory ethics training. This training should use real-world case studies, including examples of both violations and exemplary ethical behavior. This reinforces the learning and allows for discussion of new issues that may have emerged.

Create a Safe Space for Questions: Employees must feel comfortable asking questions about ethical dilemmas without fear of reprisal. A designated compliance officer or an anonymous ethics hotline can provide a safe channel for employees to seek guidance when they are unsure about the right course of action.

By combining a deep, practical understanding of the Code and Standards with a robust internal framework of preventative procedures, investment professionals can build careers and firms that not only succeed financially but also earn the lasting trust of clients and the respect of the entire industry.

Application of the Code and Standards: Level II

Upholding Integrity: An Analysis of the CFA Code and Standards

The world of finance is built on a foundation of trust. Investors place their capital, their retirement dreams, and their financial futures in the hands of professionals, expecting them to act with competence, diligence, and, above all, integrity. The CFA Institute Code of Ethics and Standards of Professional Conduct serves as the bedrock of this trust. It's not merely a set of rules to be memorized, but a comprehensive ethical framework designed to guide investment professionals in their daily actions. This framework ensures that the interests of clients are placed first, that the integrity of the capital markets is preserved, and that the profession as a whole maintains its credibility. To truly understand its application, one must move beyond theory and examine its role in practice. By evaluating a series of realistic scenarios—involving firm policies, individual conduct, and research practices—we can illuminate the fine line that often separates ethical behavior from misconduct and appreciate the profound responsibility that comes with being a CFA charterholder.

Part 1: Evaluating Practices, Policies, and Conduct

To explore the practical application of the CFA standards, let's consider a hypothetical investment firm, "Veridian Capital Management," and the conduct of its employees. By observing their practices and policies, we can begin to measure them against the stringent requirements of the Code and Standards.

Veridian has cultivated an image of success, but a closer look at its internal policies reveals a carefully curated presentation of its performance. The firm's marketing department operates under a policy that dictates all promotional materials, client brochures, and public presentations must exclusively feature the investment returns of their "Premier Growth Fund" and "Global Tech Innovators Fund." These two funds have consistently been in the top decile of their respective categories for the past five years. However, Veridian manages seven other funds, three of which have significantly underperformed their benchmarks over the same period. The policy document explicitly states the goal is to "spotlight demonstrated success and attract investors with a proven track record," thereby omitting any mention of the less successful funds. This practice presents a glowing, yet incomplete, picture of the firm's overall management capabilities.

Within the firm, we find Michael Vance, a senior portfolio manager who has built a strong network over the years. Michael has a long-standing, informal arrangement with a prominent luxury real estate agent, Julia Stone. When Michael's high-net-worth clients mention an interest in purchasing property, he consistently refers them to Julia. For every client who closes a deal with her, Julia sends Michael a case of rare, vintage wine, often valued at over a thousand dollars, delivered to his home. Michael views this as a simple gesture of gratitude between friends and professional colleagues. He has never mentioned this arrangement to his clients, believing his referrals are genuinely helpful and not influenced by the gifts. He has also never disclosed this ongoing exchange to Veridian's compliance department, considering it a personal matter unrelated to his professional duties of managing investment portfolios. His conduct, in his eyes, is separate from his fiduciary responsibilities.

Meanwhile, one of Veridian's rising research analysts, Chloe Decker, is lauded for her ability to uncover unique insights. She is currently analyzing "Innovate Pharma," a publicly traded biotechnology company. In her quest for an edge, Chloe pieces together information from several sources. First, she speaks with a former employee of a key supplier to Innovate Pharma, who complains that Innovate was consistently late on payments. Next, at an industry conference, she has a casual conversation with a mid-level marketing manager from Innovate who laments that the launch of a key new drug is facing "unexpected production hurdles," a fact not yet announced to the public. Finally, she combines these nuggets with publicly available financial reports that show a slight increase in accounts payable. Weaving these threads together, Chloe concludes that the company is facing a severe, undisclosed cash flow and production crisis. This "mosaic" of information forms the basis of her urgent "sell" recommendation, which she promptly circulates to Veridian's portfolio managers.

Lastly, there is the case of a junior trader, Ben Carter. Ben is responsible for executing large block trades for Veridian's institutional clients. He is well aware that these substantial orders often cause a predictable, short-term impact on a stock's price. Ben follows a strict personal trading rule: he will only trade for his own account after his clients' trades have been fully and completely executed. For instance, if Veridian decides to sell 500,000 shares of a particular stock, Ben diligently executes the full order. Then, observing the downward price pressure created by the large sale, he will short-sell a small number of shares in his personal account, anticipating a further slight dip. He believes this conduct is ethical because the client's order was always given absolute priority and was completed before he took any action for his own benefit. He sees it not as front-running, but as smart trading based on public market movements that he just happens to have an early insight into.

Part 2: Explaining Adherence and Violations
Evaluating the practices at Veridian Capital Management reveals significant deviations from the CFA Institute Code of Ethics and Standards of Professional Conduct. Each scenario, when analyzed through the lens of specific standards, highlights critical ethical failures.

Licensed by Google
The firm's own marketing policy is in direct violation of Standard III(D) – Performance Presentation. This standard requires that members and candidates make fair, accurate, and complete presentations of investment performance. By selectively showcasing only its top-performing funds, Veridian is creating a misleading impression of its abilities. An investor reviewing these materials would not receive a full picture of the firm's track record, which includes several underperforming funds. The omission is a material misrepresentation. The policy to "spotlight demonstrated success" is, in effect, a policy of hiding failure, which prevents potential clients from making a fully informed decision. To comply, Veridian would need to present the performance of a composite of all its funds or, at the very least, disclose that the presented performance is only for a select portion of its managed assets. The current practice is fundamentally deceptive and undermines the principle of fair dealing.

Michael Vance's referral arrangement with the real estate agent creates a cascade of violations. First, he violates Standard IV(B) – Additional Compensation Arrangements. The cases of vintage wine are clearly a form of compensation that stems from his professional role. The standard strictly requires members to not accept any gifts or compensation that could reasonably be expected to create a conflict of interest with their employer's interest unless they receive written consent from all parties involved. Michael failed to disclose the arrangement to his employer, Veridian Capital, and get their permission in writing. Secondly, he violates Standard VI(C) – Referral Fees. This standard mandates that members disclose any compensation or benefit received for the recommendation of products or services to clients. Michael's clients are unaware that their manager benefits personally from referring them to a specific agent. This disclosure is crucial because it allows the client to assess the objectivity of the referral and any potential partiality. Michael's belief that the arrangement is a private matter is incorrect; his actions create a conflict of interest that compromises his independence and objectivity.

Chloe Decker's research methods place her in a precarious position regarding Standard II(A) – Material Nonpublic Information. The "mosaic theory" allows an analyst to combine non-material public information and non-material nonpublic information to arrive at a material conclusion. Diligent research often involves uncovering small, seemingly insignificant pieces of data. However, Chloe appears to have crossed a critical line. The information from the former supplier about late payments might be considered non-material on its own. However, the tip from the marketing manager about "unexpected production hurdles" for a key drug is almost certainly material nonpublic information. Material information is anything that a reasonable investor would want to know before making an investment decision and which could significantly alter the price of the security. An unannounced production delay for a major product fits this definition perfectly. By incorporating this specific, sensitive information into her analysis and issuing a sell recommendation based on it, she is likely acting on material nonpublic information, a serious violation of the standard. Her "mosaic" is contaminated by a piece of information that was not obtained through legitimate, public means.

Finally, Ben Carter's personal trading conduct is a clear violation of Standard VI(B) – Priority of Transactions. This standard is unequivocal: investment transactions for clients and employers must have priority over investment transactions in which a member or candidate is the beneficial owner. While Ben correctly executes client trades first, he is using the knowledge of those trades and their impending market impact for his own personal gain. His actions are a form of front-running, albeit after the fact. He is profiting from information that belongs to his clients and his employer. The very knowledge of the large block trades is confidential and is an asset of the firm. By using it to inform his personal trading strategy, he is placing his own interests ahead of his duty to his employer and, by extension, its clients. The fact that the client trade is "complete" does not absolve him of his responsibility. The standard's intent is to prevent professionals from benefiting from their privileged position and knowledge of client trading activity, a principle Ben's conduct directly contravenes.

About Author

Azhar ul Haque Sario is a bestselling author and data scientist with a remarkable record of achievement. This Cambridge alumnus brings a wealth of knowledge to his work, holding an MBA, ACCA (Knowledge Level - FTMS College Malaysia and London College of Accountancy, London), BBA, and several Google certifications, including specializations in Google Data Analytics, Google Digital Marketing & E-commerce, and Google Project Management.

With ten years of business experience, Azhar combines practical expertise with his impressive academic background to craft insightful books. His prolific writing has resulted in an astounding 2810 published titles, earning him the record for the maximum Kindle editions and paperback books published by an individual author in one year, awarded by Asia Books of Records in 2024.

ORCID: https://orcid.org/0009-0004-8629-830X
Azhar.sario@hotmail.co.uk
https://www.linkedin.com/in/azharulhaquesario/

www.ingramcontent.com/pod-product-compliance
Lightning Source LLC
Chambersburg PA
CBHW020240250926
51848CB00007BA/512
9783384697363